Indian Poetics

Indian Poetics

An Introduction to Kaavyashaastra

Ravi Nandan Sinha
Narendra Kumar

Orient BlackSwan

INDIAN POETICS: AN INTRODUCTION TO KAAVYASHAASTRA

ORIENT BLACKSWAN PRIVATE LIMITED

Registered Office
3-6-752 Himayatnagar, Hyderabad 500 029, Telangana, India
e-mail: centraloffice@orientblackswan.com

Other Offices
Bengaluru, Chennai, Guwahati, Hyderabad, Kolkata, Mumbai, New Delhi, Noida, Patna, Visakhapatnam

First published 2022

ISBN 978-93-5442-109-9

035787

Typeset in Minion Pro 11/13.5 *by*
Shine Graphics, Delhi 110 094

Printed at
Yash Printographics, Greater Noida 201 310

Published by
Orient Blackswan Private Limited
3-6-752, Himayatnagar, Hyderabad 500 029, Telangana, India
e-mail: info@orientblackswan.com

Contents

In Memoriam

This book is dedicated to Dr Ravi Nandan Sinha—the professor who felt the need for a detailed yet simplified book on the subject and the dreamer who turned his wish into reality.

Sir, you may have moved on, but spiritually you remain with us and within us as a harbour light of intellect. We will miss your physical presence but will always remember a stalwart in the field of literature.

Acknowledgements

We wish to thank Fr. (Dr.) Emmanuel Baxla S.J., Director, Father Camille Bulcke Shodh Sansthan, St. Xavier's College (Autonomous), Ranchi, for his generosity in allowing us to use the library of the Institute.

For assistance in the preparation of this book we are grateful to many people, but more specifically, we would like to mention Dr Sumana Ghosh and Ms Ananya Bose of the Department of English, St. Xavier's College, Ranchi; Ms Rema Das, a PhD scholar of English; and Purwa Renu Pathak, a PG student of English, St. Xavier's College, Ranchi, who were the first readers of the manuscript and offered important feedback. We are also thankful to Professor O.P. Budholia, Professor of English at the Sanchi University of Buddhist-Indic Studies, Madhya Pradesh for his valued suggestions.

A special thanks to the publishing house, Orient BlackSwan for this book.

Postscript (by Narendra Kumar)

The world suffered many losses in the global pandemic—some passed on and others were left to mourn. Eliot once declared April as the cruellest month—this is often heard and read, but I felt its force in April 2021 when Dr R.N. Sinha passed away due to COVID-19. Many other simultaneous losses took both a mental as well as physical toll on me. I had been the silent supporter of this book while Sinha Sir took care of everything, but now it was left to me to complete the task.

With my poor technical ability and multiple health issues, I was dependent on Purwa, my daughter. The final editing and outcomes have been made possible by her efforts as well as the toil and patience of Namrata Kartik and Padmaja Anant, our associates from Orient BlackSwan. My heartfelt thanks and blessings to them.

Transliteration Chart

A Romanised transliteration system has been followed for the Sanskrit/Devanagari text in the book, with minimal use of diacritics. The transliteration system followed here may result in the Sanskrit/Devanagari text being spelt differently from more conventional spellings—for example, 'alankar' has been transliterated as 'alaNkaar'. This decision was taken to ensure that the text reads and sounds as much like the original as possible, and so that readers not familiar with transliteration systems and diacritics can pronounce these terms and phrases easily.

CONSONANTS	
Letter	**Symbol**
क	k
ख	kh
ग	g
घ	gh
च	ch
छ	chh
ज	j
झ	jh
ट	T
ठ	Th
ड	D
ढ	Dh
ण	ṇ
त	t
थ	th
द	d
ध	dh

CONSONANTS	
Letter	**Symbol**
न	n
प	p
फ	ph
ब	b
भ	bh
म	m
य	y
र	r
ल	l
व	v
श	sh
ष	Sh
स	s
ह	h
ङ	Ng
ञ	Ny
क्ष	kSh

VOWELS	
Letter	**Symbol**
अ	a
आ	aa
इ	i
ई	ee
उ	u
ऊ	oo
ए	e
ऐ	ai
ओ	o
औ	au
अं	M
अः	ah
ं	N

Pronunciation Guide

NAMES		
Spelling in Book	**Nagari**	**Pronunciation**
Abhinavagupt	अभिनवगुप्त	abhinavagupt
Anandavardhan	आनन्दवर्धन	aanandavardhan
Appaya Dikshit	अप्पैय दीक्षित	appaiyya deekShit
Ashadhar Bhatt	आशाधर भट्ट	aashaadhar bhaTT
Avantisundari	अवंतिसुन्दरी	avaNtisundaree
Avantivarma	अवंतिवर्मा	avaNtivarmaa
Bhamah	भामह	bhaamah
Bharat	भरत	bharat
Bhartrihari	भर्तृहरि	bhartrihari
Bhattalollat	भट्टलोल्लट	bhaTTalollaT
Bhattanayak	भट्टनायक	BhaTTanaayak
Bhattataut	भट्टतौत	bhaTTataut
Bhojdev	भोजदेव	bhojdev
Dandin	दण्डिन्	daṇDin
Dhananjay	धनञ्जय	dhanaNjay
Dharmakeerti	धर्मकीर्ति	dharmakeerti
Gunachandra	गुणचन्द्र	guṇachandra
Harsha	हर्षा	harShaa
Hemchandra	हेमचन्द्र	hemchandra
Jayapeed	जयापीड़	jayaapeeD
Jayadev Piyushvarsh	जयदेव पीयूषवर्ष	jayadev peeyooShvarSh
Jaydev	जयदेव (Sanskrit poeticist)	jayadev

Spelling in Book	Nagari	Pronunciation
Jayadev	जयदेव (poet and author of Geet Govindam)	jayadev
Jayaditya	जयादित्य	jayaaditya
Jeevgoswami	जीवगोस्वामी	jeevgoswaamee
Katyayan	कात्यायन	kaatyaayan
Kalhan	कल्हण	kalhaṇ
Kalidas	कालिदास	kaalidaas
Kavi Karnapur	कवि कर्णपूर	kavi karṇapoor
Keertidhar	कीर्तिधर	keertidhar
Kshemendra	क्षेमेंद्र	kShemeNdra
Lagadh	लगध	lagadh
Lalitaditya	ललितादित्य	lalitaaditya
Matrigupt	मातृगुप्त	maatrigupt
Madhusudan Saraswati	मधुसूदन सरस्वती	madhusoodan saraswatee
Mahendrapal	महेंद्रपाल	maheNdrapaal
Mahim Bhatt	महीम भट्ट	maheem bhaTT
Mahipal	महिपाल	mahipaal
Mammat	मम्मट	mammaT
Mukul Bhatt	मुकुल भट्ट	mukul bhaTT
Nandikeshwar	नंदीकेश्वर	naNdikeshwar
Narsingh Kavi	नरसिंह कवि	narsiNh kavi
Panditraj Jagannath	पंडितराज जगन्नाथ	paNDitraaj jagannaath
Panini	पाणिनि	paaṇini
Patanjali	पतञ्जलि	pataNjali
Rajanak Kuntak	राजानक कुंतक	raajaanak kuNtak
Rajshekhar	राजशेखर	raajashekhar
Ramchandra	रामचंद्र	raamachaNdra
Roopgoswami	रूपगोस्वामी	roopagoswaamee

Spelling in Book	Nagari	Pronunciation
Rudrabhatt	रुद्रभट्ट	rudrabhaTT
Rudradaman	रुद्रदामन	rudradaaman
Rudrat	रुद्रट	rudraT
Ruyyak	रुय्यक	ruyyak
Sagarnandi	सागरनंदी	saagarnaNdee
Sharadatanay	शारदातनय	shaaradaatanaya
Shobhakar Mitra	शोभाकर मित्र	shobhaakar mitra
Shrishankuk	श्रीशंकुक	shrishaNkuk
Simhavishnu	सिम्हविष्णु	simhaviShṇu
Udbhat	उद्भट	udbhaT
Vagbhatt	वाग्भट्ट	vaagbhaTT
Valmiki	वाल्मीकि	vaalmeeki
Vaman	वामन	vaaman
Vatsyayan	वात्स्यायन	vaatsyaayan
Venkata I	वेंकटा I	veNkataa I
Vidyadhar	विद्याधर	vidyaadhar
Vishwanath	विश्वनाथ	vishwanaath
Vishweshwar Pandit	विश्वेश्वर पंडित	vishweshwar paNDit
Yask	यास्क	yaask

TEXTS		
Spelling in Book	**Nagari**	**Pronunciation**
Abhidhavrittimatrika	अभिधावृत्तिमातृका	abhidhaavrittimaatrikaa
Abhinavbharati	अभिनवभारती	abhinavbhaaratee
Alankarsarsangrah	अलंकारसारसंग्रह	alaNkaarasaarsaNgraha
Alankarsarvaswa	अलंकारसर्वस्व	alaNkaarasarvaswa
Arjunacharit	अर्जुनचरित	arjunacharit
Arthashastra	अर्थशास्त्र	arthashaastra
Ashtadhyayi	अष्टाध्यायी	aShTaadhyaayee
Auchityavicharcharcha	औचित्यविचारचर्चा	auchityavichaaracharchaa
Avantisundarikatha	अवंतिसुंदरीकथा	avantisundareekathaa
Balbharat	बालभारत	baalbhaarat
Balramayana	बालरामायण	baalraamaayaṇ
Bhaktirasamritasindhu	भक्तिरसामृतसिन्धु	bhaktirasaamritasindhu
Bhamahavritti	भामहवृत्ति	bhaamahavritti
Bhamahavivaran	भामहविवरण	bhaamahavivaraṇ
Bhavprakashan	भावप्रकाशन	bhaavaprakaashan
Chandogya Upanishad	छान्दोग्योपनिषद्	chhaandogyopaniShad
Chandralok	चंद्रालोक	chaNdraalok
Chitramimansa	चित्रमीमांसा	chitrameemaaNsaa
Chitramimansakhandan	चित्रमीमांसाखण्डन	chitrameemaaNsaakhaṇDan
Dashakumaracharita	दशकुमारचरित	dashakumaaracharita
Dasharupakam	दशरूपकम्	dasharoopakaM
Devishataka	देवीशतक	deveeshataka
Dharmashastra	धर्मशास्त्र	dharmashaatra
Dharmottama	धर्मोत्तम	dharmottama
Dhwanyalok	ध्वन्यालोक	dhwanyaalok
Dhwanyaloklochan	ध्वन्यालोकलोचन	dhwanyaalokalochan
Ekawaliteeka	एकावलिटीका	ekaawaliTeekaa
Kalpasutra	कल्पसूत्र	kalpasootra
Kamashastra	कामशास्त्र	kaamashaastra

Spelling in Book	Nagari	Pronunciation
Kamasutra	कामसूत्र	kaamasootra
Karpuramanjari	कर्पूरमंजरी	karpooramaNjaree
Kavikanthabharan	कविकण्ठाभरण	kavikaṇThaabharaṇ
Kavyadarsh	काव्यादर्श	kaavyaadarsh
Kavyalankar	काव्यालंकार	kaavyaalaNkaara
Kavyalankarasarasangraha	काव्यालंकारसारसंग्रहः	kaavyaalaNkaarasaarsaNgraha
Kavyalankarsutra	काव्यालंकारसूत्र	kaavyaalaNkaarasootra
Kavyamimansa	काव्यमीमांसा	kaavyameemaaNsaa
Kavyanushasanam	काव्यानुशासनम्	kaavyaanushaasanaM
Kavyaprakash	काव्यप्रकाश	kaavyprakaasha
Kumarasambhava	कुमारसंभव	kumaarsaMbhava
Kuvalayanand	कुवलयानंद	kuvalayaanaNda
Lalitvister	ललितविस्तर	lalitavistar
Natakachandrika	नाटकचंद्रिका	naaTakachaNdrikaa
Natakalakshanaratnakosh	नाटकलक्षणरत्नकोश	naaTakalakShaṇaratnakosha
Natyadarpana	नाट्यदर्पण	naatyadarpaṇ
Natyashastra	नाट्यशास्त्र	naaTyashaastra
Nighantu	निघण्टु	nighaṇTu
Pramanavinishchaya	प्रमाणविनिश्चय	pramaaṇavinishchay
Rajatarangini	राजतरङ्गिणी	raajataraNgiṇi
Rasgangadhar	रसगंगाधर	rasagaNgaadhara
Sahityadarpan	साहित्यदर्पण	saahityadarpaṇa
Saraswatikanthabharan	सरस्वतीकण्ठाभरण	saraswateekaṇThaabharaṇa
Shatapatha Brahmana	शतपथब्राह्मण	shatapathbraahmaṇa
Shringarprakash	शृङ्गारप्रकाश	shriNgaaraprakaash
Shringaratilak	शृङ्गारतिलक	shriNgaaratilak
Subhashitani	सुभाषितानि	subhaaShitaani
Sundarkaand	सुंदरकाण्ड	suNdarakaaṇD
Suvrittatilak	सुवृत्ततिलक	suvrittatilak
Trivenika	त्रिवेणिका	triveṇikaa

Spelling in Book	Nagari	Transliteration
Ujjwalanilamani	उज्ज्वलनीलमणि	ujjwalaneelamaṇi
Uttarkaand	उत्तरकांड़	uttarakaaND
Vagbhattalankar	वागभट्टालंकार	vaagbhaTTaalaNkaar
Vakroktijeevit	वक्रोक्तिजीवित	vakroktijeevit
Vakyapadiyam	वाक्यपदीयम्	vaakyapadeeyam
Venisamhara	वेणीसंहार	veṇeesaMhaara
Viddhashalabhanjika	विद्धशालभंजिका	viddhashaalabhaNjikaa
Vikramorvashiyam	विक्रमोर्वशीयम्	vikramorvasheeyam
Vishambanaleela	विषमबाणलीला	viShambaaṇaleelaa
Vrittavartika	वृत्तवार्तिक	vrittavaartika
Vyaktivivek	व्यक्तिविवेक	vyaktivivek
Yogashastra	योगशास्त्र	yogashaastra

Preface

The scope of Indian poetics is extremely vast and though there are many excellent books on it, very few of them are in English. In most Indian universities, students of English literature have to study Indian poetics as one of their courses and have felt the need for a concise yet comprehensive book on the subject. This book aims to fulfill that need.

The present book deals with all the major topics in Indian poetics and also places them in the larger context of the history of the growth of aesthetics in India. Emphasis has been laid on explaining complex concepts in simple language. Wherever necessary, quotations from primary texts have been given. To assist the student, the main points in a chapter have been summarised in the form of tables.

Beginning with Acharya Bharat, the contribution of major Indian scholars has been discussed in the chapter after the Introduction. Chapter 3 deals with the features of poetry, causes of poetic creation, the purpose of writing poetry, the qualities of poetry and various kinds of poetry. The fourth chapter is concerned with modes of signification and syntax. The next six chapters deal with the six major theories in Indian poetics, which are Rasa, AlaNkaar, Reeti, Dhwani, Vakrokti and Auchitya. The final chapter is on flaws in poetry. This is followed by a glossary of Sanskrit terms used in the book. We hope that readers will find this book an aid in understanding the history, evolution and scope of Indian poetics.

Ravi Nandan Sinha
Narendra Kumar

1

Introduction

Indian poetics has a rich and almost unbroken intellectual tradition of reading and interpreting literature of over two thousand years. Our ancient scholars wrote on the theory and practice of literature not only in Sanskrit, but also in other old Indian languages such as Pali and Tamil. In its comprehensiveness and sophistication, Indian poetics can be compared with similar bodies of knowledge elsewhere in the world, such as the poetics of ancient Greece and Rome. Yet, our poetics is uniquely Indian. It is closely related to the language, philosophy, religion and world view of ancient Indians.

Indian poetics has some easily recognisable features. First, it is extremely comprehensive and there is hardly any aspect of literature which it does not cover. It even discusses the flaws or mistakes that occur in poetry—something which is not commonly seen elsewhere. A second unique feature of Indian poetics is its focus on the reader of literature. From the very beginning, our scholars focused on the cultivated reader, the sahridaya, while discussing theories of literature. For example, the theory of rasa is based entirely on the reader's response to kaavya (poetry or drama). A third thing that strikes us about Indian poetics is that unlike classical European literary theory, our theory is closely linked with linguistics and grammar and its contribution to semantics is considerable. Further, in discussing literary phenomena, our scholars display an encyclopedic range of knowledge and are capable of making extremely fine and subtle distinctions between various elements of literature.

An important feature of note in Indian poetics is the presence of various schools of thought or sampradaays during its long history. There are six such schools: Rasa, AlaNkaar, Dhwani, Reeti, Vakrokti and Auchitya. Some scholars are of the view that there are more than six schools, but these six are generally considered to be the major ones. There have been periods in which a particular school of thought predominated the study of poetics. Followers of a particular school have argued that a specific literary theory, such as rasa or alaNkaar or dhwani, is more important than other theories. For example, a rasavaadi aachaarya (a follower of the Rasa School) argues that rasa is the soul or essence of poetry.

The scholar who first established the centrality of a particular theory is regarded as the founder of that school. For example, Kuntak, who established the view that vakrokti is the essence of poetry, is regarded as the founder of the Vakrokti School. But there is a contrary view which says that it is not right to think of the history of Indian poetics only in terms of schools. It is said that mere emphasis on a particular literary principle cannot form a school, nor can a single writer without followers constitute a movement. To support this contention, examples of scholars like Dandin are given. As Dandin emphasises both alaNkaar and guṇa, it is difficult to place him in any particular school. Again, Kshemendra, who is called the founder of the Auchitya School, did not have any major followers after him. Should then the theory of auchitya be called a separate school? It is a debatable point but traditionally, Indian poetics has been discussed in terms of these schools of thought.

Acharya Bharat's *Natyashastra* is regarded as the first available text on Indian poetics. Written around the second century BCE, it deals primarily with drama (naaTya means drama). It concerns itself with almost all aspects of dramatic presentation including dance, music, acting and even the structure of a stage. Thus, the journey of Indian poetics began with dramaturgy, but as time went on all genres of literature were included in its ambit. *Natyashastra* is a very important work. Much of the theory discussed in *Natyashastra* became the point of departure for later scholars. Indian classical dance forms such as Bharatnatyam draw their vocabulary and grammar from Bharat's work. We will have more to say about Bharat and other scholars in the next chapter.

Indian poetics has multiple concerns. Some of these topics have been discussed by every theorist while some others have been looked at only by a few writers. All scholars of Indian poetics have paid close attention to the distinguishing features (lakShaṇs) of kaavya or poetry. They have tried to identify the elements that separate poetry from non-poetry. They have also discussed the prayojan (purpose or object) of writing and of reading poetry, as well. From the beginning, scholars have commented on alaNkaars or figures of speech and have debated its relative importance in poetry. The guṇas (qualities) of poetry have also been studied by all scholars. Along with the guṇas they have also enumerated and analysed the doShas or flaws in poetry. Finally, the types of poetry have also been explained by every scholar.

There are some scholars who are known for their contribution to a particular field of study. For instance, Bharat in his *Natyashastra* discusses topics which are mainly related to drama, such as rasa, acting, music, dance and similar other subjects. On the other hand, Bhamah's *Kavyalankar,* Vaman's *Kavyalankarsutra*, Rudrat's *Kavyalankar*, Mammat's *Kavyaprakash* and Panditraj Jagannath's *Rasgangadhar* deal with various aspects of poetry but not specifically with drama. Kshemendra's *Auchityavicharcharcha* is chiefly concerned with the theory of auchitya. Udbhat's *Alankarsarsangrah*, Ruyyak's *Alankarsarvaswa* and Appaya Dikshit's *Kuvalayanand* deal primarily with alaNkaars. Anandavardhan's *Dhwanyalok* and Kuntak's *Vakroktijeevit* are concerned with dhwani and vakrokti respectively.

In the course of its long history, a number of terms such as kaavyashaastra, alaNkaarshaastra, saahityashaastra and kriyaakalp have been used for Indian poetics. Scholars belonging to a particular age preferred a particular term and used it in the titles of their works. In sixth century BCE, when Bhamah wrote his seminal work on poetics, he chose to call it *Kaavyalankar*, using the words 'kaavya' (poetry) and 'alaNkaar' (ornament) in the title. Again, when Dandin wrote his *Kavyadarsh* he also used the term kaavya in the title. In the ninth century, we have Vaman and Rudrat, two great scholars of Indian poetics, both of whom gave the same title to their books and called them *Kavyalankar*. Later, in the eleventh century Mammat wrote a book on poetics and called it *Kavyaprakash* or 'The light of poetry'. In the fourteenth century Vishwanath used the term 'saahitya' for poetry and called his work *Sahityadarpan*, or

'The mirror of literature'. In the titles of all these books, words like kaavya, shaastra, saahitya and alaNkaar appear frequently, and therefore, it is necessary to know what they mean.

Kaavya ordinarily means 'poetry' but in Sanskrit poetics the term is used to denote all kinds of creative literature, that is, poetry, prose and drama. Etymologically, kaavya is derived from kavi (poet) and so kaavya means the work of a kavi. Defining kaavya in his *Dhwanyaloklochan*, Abhinavagupt writes, 'कवनीयं काव्यम्' ('kavaneeyam kaavyam'): whatever a kavi does is kaavya. Vidyadhar in his *Ekawaliteeka* also says that kaavya is the karma (activity) of a poet. The word 'kavi' itself may have been derived either from the root word 'kav' or 'ku'. If kavi has come from 'kav', it denotes a thoughtful person of great knowledge and talent. That person is also gifted with the ability to describe something in a lively manner. If, however, 'ku' is taken to be the root word for kavi, it denotes a person who speaks because 'ku' means 'to make a sound' or 'to talk'. Kavi, therefore, is a person who has a great deal of knowledge about things and is endowed with the power to express sentiments and emotions in words. So, whatever such a person writes is kaavya.

And indeed, Indian scholars believe that it is essential for a poet to be a well read person. Rajshekhar in his *Kavyamimansa* says a poet should be familiar with the principles of literary creation or kaavyashaastra. He says that as one cannot know the presence of things in the absence of light, one cannot write poetry without knowing kaavyashaastra. But for a poet it is not enough to know poetics, he is expected to be familiar with all the Vedas, Puranas, Shastras and the vidyaa's or various arts. Rajshekhar says that a poet should also have knowledge about this world and the world beyond. He should be familiar with the geography of various regions, their cultures and ways of life. He should also know how these things change, their climate and their flora and fauna.

The other word in kaavyashaastra is 'shaastra' which in Sanskrit has multiple meanings, some of which are 'order', 'command', 'rule' and 'method'. Shaastra, therefore, normally means a text that lays down rules about something. By implication, it also means a text which describes the right methodology for studying and writing about a subject. Shaastra also means a compilation of knowledge about a particular subject. For instance, we have words like vedaaNtashaastra, tarkashaastra, arthashaastra and others, which mean the science of VedaaNta, logic and economics respectively. Thus, kaavyashaastra should mean a set of explicit regulations and principles that govern the art of literary composition. The term was first used by Bhojdev, the eleventh century scholar–king who wrote *Saraswatikanthabharan*, in which he says that the primary function of kaavyashaastra is to lay down the rules of literary composition. Every scholar, however, does not think that the laying down of rules is the only function of a shaastra. Vishweshwar, the famous commentator on Mammat's *Kavyaprakash*, believes that the function of shaastra is not merely to lay down rules; it should also deal with other weighty matters related to the subject.

Saahityashaastra is another term used for poetics, the word 'saahitya' being a synonym for kaavya. Saahitya comes from one of the earliest definitions of poetry given by Bhamah who famously wrote:

> शब्दार्थौ सहितौ काव्यं गद्यं पद्यं च तद्द्विधा,
> संस्कृतं प्राकृतं चान्यदपभ्रंशमिति त्रिधा। (*काव्यालंकार*)
>
> shabdaarthausahitaukaavyam gadyam padyam cha taddvidha,
> saNskritaM praakritaM chaanyadapbhraMshamiti tridhaa |
> (*Kavyalankar*)
>
> A togetherness (or fusion) of shabda (word) and artha (meaning) is called poetry. It is of two kinds, prose and verse. It is further classified into three types: Sanskrit, Prakrit and Apabhramsh.

In this definition, the word 'sahit' means 'being together'. Poetry is created when the shabda and its artha are fused (sahit) into one. The noun 'saahitya' has been derived from 'sahit' and means poetry or creative literature in general. The implicit meaning of this definition is that poetry is a fusion of form and content. But can all combinations of shabda and artha be called poetry? If we accept this definition even non–literary writing will have to be called saahitya. Therefore, Bhamah qualifies this definition by saying that only that combination of shabda and artha is poetry which has been embellished by alaNkaars and so has acquired beauty. It should also provide aesthetic pleasure or aanaNd to the reader. Later, Kuntak also used the terms kaavya and saahitya synonymously. In the ninth century, Rajshekhar used the terms 'saahityavichaar' (contemplation on poetry) and 'saahityashaastra' (treatise on poetry) to denote poetics.

Scholars have also used the term 'alaNkaarshaastra', or the science of alanNkaars, for poetics. In a literal sense, 'alaNkaar' means 'ornament', 'embellishment' or 'adornment' but when applied to literature it refers to poetic figures of speech and literary devices. It is one of the most commonly used terms for poetics, probably because early writers like Bhamah considered alaNkaar to be the most important element in poetic expression. In the earliest phase of the history of Sanskrit poetics, many leading scholars used the word alaNkaar in the titles of their books, as we have seen above. During that period, the primary yardstick for evaluating the excellence of poetic composition was the quality and richness of alaNkaars used in it.

Another term used for poetics is 'kriyaakalp', which literally means the technique of literary creation. This term was commonly used before the time of Bhamah and Dandin and seems to be the ancient name for poetics—this is the term we come across in the epics and Puranas. Vishweshwar thinks that this term is perhaps the shortened version of kaavyakriyaakalp, another name for kaavyashaastra. *Lalitvister*, an important Buddhist text, uses kriyaakalp instead of kaavyashaastra and Vatsyayan in his *Kamasutra* mentions kriyaakalp as one among the sixty-four arts. In the *Uttarkaand* of Valmiki's Ramayana also we find the use of both 'kriyaakalpavid' and 'kaavyavid' to describe a person who knows the art of writing poetry. Again, Udbhat in his *Bhamahvivaran* uses the word kriyaa to describe the act of writing poetry, and for Kalidas kriyaa is synonymous with drama.

Indian poetics did not develop in a vacuum. It has borrowed concepts from other intellectual disciplines such as Darshan, Vyaakaraṇ, Nyaay, MimaaNsa, VedaaNta, SaNkhya, and so on. Darshan means philosophy. Vyaakaraṇ is the Sanskrit word for grammar and Acharya Panini's *Ashtadhyayi* is commonly regarded as the greatest work of Sanskrit grammar. Anandavardhan says that grammarians are great scholars and grammar is the source of all knowledge. Nyaay means 'rule', 'judgement' or 'method'. It is one of the six schools of Hindu philosophy. Nyaay is fundamentally concerned with logic and epistemology, especially that which deals with the methods, scope and validity of acquiring knowledge. MimaaNsa means 'critical investigation' and refers to the study of and reflection on the meaning of early Vedic texts. VedaaNta, also known as 'Uttar MimaaNsa' ('uttar' means 'later'), deals with philosophical ideas contained in the later Vedic texts, that is, the Upanishads. SaNkhya deals with issues related to the process of gaining knowledge. It is a dualistic philosophy that sees the universe as made up of PuruSh (consciousness or energy) and Prakriti (matter). We should remember that ancient literary theorists were familiar with all these branches of learning and borrowed ideas from them while formulating and discussing their theories of literature. Hence, it sometimes becomes necessary to understand a point in Hindu philosophy or Sanskrit grammar in order to understand a principle in Indian poetics.

Every ancient Indian poet understood that knowledge of kaavyashaastra was as important to him as his ability to write poetry. In his *Kavyamimansa*, Rajshekhar calls kaavyashaastra the seventh vedaaNg. According to the conventional classification of Hindu knowledge there are six vedaaNgs, or fundamental disciplines of study. Literally, 'vedaaNg' means 'limbs of the Veda'—ShikShaa, Kalp, Vyaakaraṇ, Nirukt, JyotiSh and ChhaNdashaastra. ShikShaa is a Sanskrit word which means 'instruction', 'learning', 'lesson' or 'learning a skill' and as a vedaaNg it deals with the phonology of Sanskrit. Kalp refers to the field of study that focuses on procedures and ceremonies related to Vedic ritual practices. Max Mueller, the German Indologist, calls it 'the ceremonial'. In Hinduism, the *Kalpasutras* are the major texts of Kalp vedaaNg. These texts describe Vedic rituals and those associated with various rites of passage such as birth, weddings and death. These texts also describe the proper conduct and duties of an individual. Vyaakaraṇ is concerned with rules of grammar and linguistics. Panini and Yask were two of the greatest grammarians of ancient India. The discipline of Nirukt covers the etymology and correct interpretation of Sanskrit words used in the Vedas. Nirukt offers a glossary and discusses how archaic and uncommon words in the Vedas can be understood. Yask, who is the most celebrated scholar of Nirukt, lived in about the fifth century and wrote *Nighantu*, the first book on the subject. JyotiSh is a science which deals with astronomy and *Vedanga jyotish* is the earliest known Indian text on astronomy. Tradition has it that it was written by Lagadh. Most scholars believe that the text was written between 1400 and 1200 BCE. ChhaNdashaastra deals with prosody. To this list of six vedaaNgs, Rajshekhar added kaavyashaastra and believed that for acquiring a comprehensive knowledge of literature it is necessary not only to study it, but also to understand the principles behind it. He says in his *Kavyamimansa*, 'The *Acharyas* have discovered the six disciplines of *ShikSha*, *Kalp*, *Vyaakaran*, *Nirukta*, *Chhand* and *Jyotish*. Because it helps in the study of these six *Vedangas*, *alankarshastra* is the seventh field of study'. Here alaNkaarshaastra is a synonym for kaavyashaastra. This shows the importance kaavyashaastra had in the education system of ancient India.

2

The Tradition of Indian Poetics

- Major scholars
- Schools of Indian poetics

The Indian tradition of formulating and analysing the principles of literary writing goes back at least two thousand years. It began with Acharya Bharat around the second century BCE, if not earlier, and flowed continuously down to the seventeenth century when Panditraj Jagannath, a contemporary of the Mughal Emperor Shahjahan, wrote his *Rasgangadhar*. Even after the seventeenth century, texts on poetics were written but the most important work in the area had already been done. The greatest scholars of the field had already written their works—scholars such as Bharat, Bhamah, Dandin, Vaman, Rudrat, Anandavardhan, Rajshekhar, Abhinavagupt, Rajanak Kuntak, Kshemendra, Mammat, Vishwanath and Panditraj Jagannath.

It was also the period during which all the major theories in poetics were formulated: rasa, alaNkaar, reeti, vakrokti, dhwani and auchitya. The theory of rasa tried to understand how literature evokes emotions in the reader. Scholars of the AlaNkaar School were concerned primarily with the various literary devices that a poet uses. Reeti dealt with poetic diction and vakrokti studied the nature of poetic expression. The Dhwani School was interested in understanding how poetry can suggest more than it says. This theory introduced the element of imagination into literary discussion. Finally, the theory of auchitya considered the elements of consistency and harmony in poetry. These six theories constitute the six major schools of Indian poetics.

Although there is some debate about when the history of Indian poetics began, it is commonly accepted that Acharya Bharat, or

Bharat Muni as he is sometimes called, was the first major scholar of Indian poetics. He wrote *Natyashastra* which is regarded as a seminal text on the subject. It is not improbable, though, that even before him books on poetics were written. In fact, Bharat himself refers to some earlier writers such as a scholar named Acharya Nandikeshwar. Details of his life and work are only vaguely known to us and a great deal of it forms the stuff of legend. For instance, he has been called a disciple of Lord Shiva. It is said that Shiva was a great exponent of yoga, dance, drama, music, tantra, *mimaaNsa* and kaamasutra and was Bharat's teacher. Thus, texts on poetics might have been written before Bharat but are not available to us now.

However, terms associated with literary analysis may be found even in the *Rigveda*, the oldest of all the Vedas. In the *Rigveda*, we find terms like rasa and alaNkaar which tells us that even in those days, people were familiar with the technical aspects of poetry. In the *Rigveda*, the term 'rasa' has been used to denote the implicit meaning of an expression while 'alaNkaar' refers to that language which has been embellished with literary devices. In later literature also, we find similar terms used. For example, there are references to alaNkaars in the *Yajurveda* and the *Samaveda*, and also in some of the Upanishads, Brahmanas and other similar texts. The *Chandogya Upanishad* and the *Shatapatha Brahmana*, for example, mention alaNkaar repeatedly. Yask, who was an ancient lexicographer of Sanskrit, has discussed the types and features of upamaa or simile, in his book *Nighantu* which is a lexicon of rare and difficult words collected by ancient Indian sages in order to understand Vedic texts. In Valmiki's Ramayana as well the nine rasas are mentioned. Again, in the books of grammar by Panini, Katyayan and Patanjali there are occasional references to terms associated with poetics. Further, a rock inscription of King Rudradaman of Junagarh (150CE) distinguishes between prose and verse which suggests that such a distinction between these forms had already been established. The inscription is written in ornate prose and praises King Rudradaman as a writer of powerful poetry and prose. It adds that his writing is sweet, satisfying and full of alaNkaars, besides having many other literary qualities. On the basis of all this, we can say that from the time of the earliest

Vedic texts to Bharat, Indian scholars were familiar with the basic concepts of poetics.

Although some scholars have traced the beginnings of poetics to Vedic literature, it will be erroneous to think that the Vedas discuss literary theory as an independent discipline. The mere fact that terms related to poetics were used in the Vedas, or that the term 'upamaa' appears there, is not sufficient evidence to prove that Vedic literature discusses poetics. Similarly, in ancient Sanskrit grammar there are references to poetics but in these texts the focus is on grammar and not on poetics. Thus, these occasional references to literary devices in pre-Bharat texts are neither comprehensive nor focused enough to constitute a systematic study of poetics. It is possible that there was no systematic study of the subject, or if there was, we have lost those books. Therefore, Bharat's *Natyashastra* is taken to be the first book of Indian poetics.

MAJOR SCHOLARS

Bharat

Bharat (second century BCE) has been mentioned by almost all later Indian scholars. So, it is clear that he came before all of them and was important enough to be referred frequently. His *Natyashastra* is the oldest comprehensive work on Indian poetics though even before it, as mentioned earlier, references to elements of literature were made in various other texts including the *Rigveda*.

We do not know whether *Natyashastra* is the work of one author or of a number of authors who kept adding to it for centuries. Attempts have been made to determine the age in which Bharat lived. Professor A.B. Keith (1879–1944), a Scottish scholar of Sanskrit, thought that Bharat could not have lived before the third century BCE. Professor Harprasad Shastri (1853–1931), professor of Sanskrit at Dhaka University, on the other hand believed that Bharat belonged to second century BCE. In *The Sourcebook of Indian Civilization*, Nihar Ranjan Ray thinks that *Natyashastra* in its present form may not be older than the fifth or sixth century CE. It can only mean that later scholars kept revising *Natyashastra*, but in its original form this seminal work on dramaturgy was written at least two thousand years ago. The importance of this book is evident from the fact that Kalidas, perhaps the greatest dramatist in Sanskrit literature, refers to it in his play *Vikramorvashiyam*. Acharya Panini, author of *Ashtadhyayi* and certainly the greatest Sanskrit grammarian, also mentions Bharat with great reverence.

Whatever be the age in which it was written, all scholars agree that *Natyashastra* is one of the most important texts in Indian poetics. The book is written in the form of dialogues and comprises thirty-six chapters (though one edition published by Kavyamala, Mumbai in 1894 has thirty-seven chapters). According to ancient commentators there are only thirty-six chapters in the book. These thirty-six chapters have six thousand shloks (verses) which fall into three categories: sootra, bhaaShya and kaarikaa. A 'sootra' is a short sentence defining something; 'bhaaShya' means 'an explanation'; and 'kaarikaa' is a short verse explaining a literary principle in the least number of words possible and is meant to be memorised by the student.

The scope of *Natyashastra* is vast and almost everything related to drama has been discussed in it. Although written primarily in verse, Bharat has used prose in the sixth, seventh and twenty-seventh chapters. In this text, we have a detailed discussion of acting, dance, music, musical instruments, stagecraft, rasas (emotions experienced by the spectators during a dramatic presentation), rules of versification, alaNkaars, and even the structure of the stage and the auditorium. It also comments on various aspects of poetry such as alaNkaars, guṇas (excellences or qualities of poetry), doShas (flaws in poetry) and lakShaṇs (characteristic features of poetry). However, we must remember that it is primarily a book on dramaturgy. Bharat rates drama very highly and believes that it includes all genres of literature. He says, 'There is no knowledge, no skill, no art, no yoga and no action that is not displayed in drama'.

A number of commentaries on *Natyashastra* were written but one of the most frequently mentioned is Abhinavagupt's *Abhinavbharati*. Other commentators on *Natyashastra* include

Udbhat, Lollat, Shrishankuk, Bhattanayak, Keertidhar and Matrigupt. In the seventh century, Harsha (606–647 CE), a Hindu emperor of northern India, also wrote a commentary on *Natyashastra*.

Bhamah

For almost eight centuries after Bharat, we do not know of any major scholar of Indian poetics. It is only in the sixth century that Bhamah's *Kavyalankar* ('Ornament of poetry') appears. He occupies a central place in the history of Indian poetics as it was he who established an independent tradition of discussion on alaNkaar and guṇa for the first time. During the same period, we have grammarians such as Yask, Panini and Patanjali who also discuss alaNkaar. Thus, the centrality of rasa which Bharat had established was disturbed to some extent and alaNkaar remained at the centre of literary discussions for a fairly long time after Bhamah.

Not much is known about Bhamah's life but, in all probability, he belonged to today's Kashmir region. Some believe that he was a Buddhist, though that is a moot point. From the last verse of his *Kavyalankar* we know only that the name of his father was Rakrilgomin. Bhamah is one of those scholars who have been frequently quoted by later writers.

Bhamah's *Kavyalankar* is divided into six chapters and contains four hundred verses. The opening chapter of the book deals with such topics as the purpose (prayojan) of poetry, the qualities of a poet and the characteristics and types of poetry. The second chapter deals with the qualities or excellences (guṇas) of poetry and alaNkaars (poetic devices) such as anupraas (alliteration) and upamaa (simile). An important thing to remember about Bhamah is that he differed from Bharat in a fundamental sense when he reduced the number of guṇas mentioned by Bharat. Bharat asserts in his *Natyashastra* that there are ten guṇas, while Bhamah says that there are only three: maadhurya (sweetness), oja (strength and energy) and prasaad (lucidity). We shall explore the guṇas later. The third chapter is about the remaining twenty-three arthaalaNkaars (alaNkaars related to meaning). In the fourth chapter Bhamah discusses ten kinds of doShas or flaws in poetry and also gives examples. The fifth chapter is concerned with the eleventh doSha and illustrates it with examples. The final chapter is on the use of vocabulary.

Although lacking a well-defined structure, *Kavyalankar* offers some very useful insights into the nature of poetry. The first commentary on *Kavyalankar* was Udbhat's *Bhamahavritti* or *Bhamahavivaran* written in the ninth century. Later, Anandavardhan also mentions Bhamah in his *Dhwanyalok* and Abhinavagupt refers to him while discussing the characteristics of poetry.

Bhamah is the earliest scholar of the AlaNkaar School of poetics. One of his greatest contributions to the subject is that he was the first scholar to attempt a definition of poetry. Poetry, according to him, is a fusion of shabda (word) and artha (meaning). He writes:

शब्दार्थौ सहितौ काव्यम् । (*काव्यालंकार*)

shabdaarthau sahitau kaavyam I (*Kavyalankar*)

Poetry is the fusion of word and meaning.

We shall have more to say about this definition in a later chapter.

Dandin

After Bhamah, another major scholar was Dandin. He was said to be a part of the court of the Pallava king Simhavishnu, who ruled over a large part of southern India. It is said that his ancestors had migrated from modern day Gujarat to South India. There is a great deal of speculation about which era Dandin belonged to. Scholars such as Max Mueller and Albrecht Weber, a German Indologist, believed that he belonged to the sixth century CE, while Hermann Jacobi and Peter Peterson, the Scottish professor of Oriental Languages and Sanskrit at Elphinstone College, Mumbai, believed that he belonged to the early part of the seventh century, which is a view generally accepted today.

We know about three books that Dandin wrote. They are *Kavyadarsh*, a book on poetics, *Dashakumaracharita* and *Avantisundarikatha* (the latter two being works of prose). His *Kavyadarsh* shows the influence of Bhamah but in his treatment of guṇas, rasa, vakrokti and many other alaNkaars he differs with his predecessor. *Kavyadarsh* deals with subjects such as the characteristics of poetry, types of poetry, reeti (style or diction), guṇas, alaNkaar and flaws in poetry. The book is divided into three chapters and contains a total of six hundred and sixty verses. In the first chapter, Dandin deals with topics such as the definition of poetry, types of poetry, features of different kinds of poetry, various kinds of prose literature, reeti, guṇas and the qualities of a poet. In the second and third chapters he discusses various kinds of alaNkaars. Like Bhamah, Dandin also belongs to the AlaNkaar School of poetics because he considers alaNkaar to be the core element of poetry.

A notable feature of *Kavyadarsh* is that it discusses the features of a mahaakaavya (epic) in considerable detail. Dandin states that the epic begins with an invocation to the deities. The story of an epic is divided into sargas (sections) and that the sargas must be of almost equal length. The basis of the story must be either some historical event or some other suitable tale. The epic must describe a variety of events and happenings. The hero of the epic must be a man of extremely noble character and the story must include events like meeting, parting, marriage, birth of the prince, sending a messenger to the antagonist, campaign against the antagonist, the ensuing battle, and the final victory of the hero. The verse in an epic must evoke rasas and must be striking in its description. Dandin goes on to say that even if an epic lacks any one of these elements, it can still be called an epic if it is capable of evoking rasas in the reader. In *Kavyadarsh* Dandin also describes the features of the prose narrative and mentions two kinds—kathaa and aakhyaayikaa.

Vaman

Like Bhamah, Vaman is a scholar about whom we know very little. We know that he belonged to the present day region of Kashmir who lived either in the second half of the eighth century CE or in the early part of the ninth century. Kalhan writes in his *Rajatarangini* that Vaman was a minister in the court of Jayaditya, the king of Kashmir. *Rajatarangini*, or 'The river of kings', was written in the twelfth century CE and is a verse chronicle of the history and legends of the northwestern part of India, especially of present day Kashmir. This book mentions Vaman as a great scholar.

Vaman's name is associated with the theory of reeti. His *Kavyalankarsutra* is the seminal text on reeti. As its name suggests, the book is written in the form of sootras (a sootra is a short and terse description of a literary principle) and is the first book of Indian poetics to be written in that style. Besides the sootras, the book also has vrittis (explanations) and udaaharaṇs (examples). The sootras and vrittis are written by Vaman himself but the examples have been taken from other writers. The book is divided into five sections with a total of over three hundred sootras. The first section is divided into three chapters which deal with topics such as the characteristic features of poetry, the purpose of writing and reading poetry, causes of poetic creation and reeti. The second section deals with flaws in poetry and the third with guṇas of poetry. The third section also discusses alaNkaars. The fourth section is also about alaNkaars and the last section deals with vocabulary. Although *Kavyalankarsutra* discusses a number of topics, its primary focus is on alaNkaars.

Vaman considers reeti the core constituent of poetry. In his *Kavyalankarsutra* he says, 'Reetiraatmakaavyasya' which means, 'Reeti is the soul of poetry'. Reeti, as we know, refers to the style of writing, and Vaman identified three main reetis—vaidarbhee, gauDee and paaNcaalee. We shall discuss these reetis at some length in Chapter 7. Another important contribution of Vaman is that he discussed the difference between alaNkaar and guṇas with great lucidity.

Udbhat

Bhamah, Dandin and Udbhat are the three greatest scholars of the AlaNkaar School. Udbhat's full name was Bhattodbhat. We learn from Kalhan's *Rajatarangini* that he was the chief scholar of the court of King Jayapeed of Kashmir who ruled in the closing decades of the eighth century. From one of the verses of *Rajatarangini* it appears that as a scholar, Udbhat was highly respected by the king who, it is said, paid him a salary of one lakh dinars. It may be an exaggeration, but it certainly tells us how important Udbhat's position was in the king's court.

Udbhat wrote *Kavyalankarsarasangrah* (a book on poetics), *Bhamahavivaran* (a commentary on Bhamah's *Kavyalankar*) and

Kumarasambhava (a narrative poem based on Kalidas's famous epic *Kumarasambhavam*). His *Kavyalankarasarsangrah*, divided into six sections, is an important text describing various kinds of alaNkaars. In his discussion on alaNkaars he is heavily indebted to Bhamah but we cannot call him a slavish imitator. For instance, unlike Bhamah, he does not consider some alaNkaars such as upamaa, roopak and utprekShaa to be independent alaNkaars.

Rudrat

Rudrat is another major literary theorist about whose life we know very little. All we can say is that he lived in the ninth century and most probably belonged to the present day Kashmir region like Udbhat. It is interesting to note that for about five hundred years after Bhamah, this region remained a very important centre for the study of poetics. We find that a majority of the greatest scholars of kaavyashaastra were from what we know as Kashmir.

Although Rudrat's *Kavyalankar* deals with many other topics which were commonly discussed in books on poetics, its primary focus is on alaNkaars. A fairly long book with sixteen chapters, it deals with a number of issues related to various aspects of poetry such as the purpose of poetry, factors which cause poetry to be written, and the features, forms and defects of poetry. The book also has a section on words and various modes of signification.

Rudrat's greatest contribution to Indian poetics is that he is the first scholar to offer a classification of alaNkaars which was much more comprehensive that what had been attempted before. He mentions a large number of alaNkaars, their types and subtypes. But he did not ignore the importance of rasa in poetry and the last four chapters of his book are concerned with rasa. While Bharat has mentioned only eight rasas, Rudrat believed that there were ten in all. We could say that among the works devoted primarily to a study of alaNkaars, Rudrat's *Kavyalankar* is the first text to discuss rasa in such comprehensive detail. He elaborates on the meaning of rasa and instead of confining it to drama, he sees it as a feature of all kinds of literature. In his *Kavyalankar*, he goes to the extent of declaring that poetry without rasa is not fit to be called poetry.

Table 2.1: Scholars from Bharat to Rudrat

Scholar	Century	Works	Main contribution
Bharat	2nd cent. BCE	*Natyashastra*	writes extensively on the theory of rasa, drama, acting, music and dance
Bhamah	6th cent. CE	*Kavyalankar*	the first major scholar of the AlaNkaar School; first to define poetry: 'shabdaarthau sahitau kaavyam'.
Dandin	7th cent. CE	*Kavyadarsh*	writes primarily on alaNkaars
Vaman	8th cent. CE	*Kavyalankarsutra*	writes primarily on alaNkaars
Udbhat	8th cent. CE	*Kavyalankarsarasangrah Bhamahavivaran*	writes primarily on alaNkaars
Rudrat	9th cent. CE	*Kavyalankar*	writes primarily on alaNkaars

Rajanak Anandavardhan

A scholar of the ninth century, Anandavardhan also comes from the modern day region of Kashmir is a major name in the history of Indian poetics. Kalhan's *Rajatarangini* tells us that he was a contemporary of King Avantivarma of Kashmir who gave him the title of 'Rajanak', conferred only on the most prominent scholars of the time. Avantivarma ruled in the latter half of the ninth century and therefore we conclude that Anandavardhan must also belong to the same period. Besides *Dhwanyalok*, his masterpiece, he also wrote a number of books such as *Arjunacharit*, *Vishambanaleela*, *Devishataka* and *Dharmottama*. This last book is a work of philosophy and is a profound commentary on *Pramanavinishchaya*, Dharmakeerti's work on Buddhist philosophy. Anandavardhan was, thus, not only a scholar of poetics but also a poet and philosopher of the first order.

Anandavardhan's name is associated with the theory of dhwani which he propounded in his seminal text *Dhwanyalok*. He is considered to be the founder of what came to be known as the Dhwani School of Indian poetics. *Dhwanyalok* literally means

'The light of dhwani' and seems to suggest that without the element of dhwani, poetry is without light. Dhwani is that characteristic of poetry to suggest more than what it literally says. In this book, Anandavardhan discusses various elements of poetry but subsumes all of them under the rubric of dhwani.

Dhwanyalok is divided into four sections called udyots. The first udyot/section examines the arguments given by earlier scholars who tried to prove that dhwani, or the suggestive power of language, is not the central defining feature of poetry. It is in this section that he considers dhwani to be the fundamental element of poetry. In the second udyot, he discusses various types of dhwani, the nature of rasa, the guṇas of poetry and explains the difference between dhwani and alaNkaars. The third udyot once again takes up the nature and kinds of dhwani and offers a comprehensive account of the idea. In the fourth and final udyot, he describes the attributes of a poet and also shows how dhwani can be used as a valid principle and methodology for the interpretation of a literary text.

Rajshekhar

An important scholar of the tenth century, Rajshekhar belonged to the present day region of Maharashtra and his family was known by the name of Yayawar. He was the guru of King Mahendrapaal (c. 885–910 CE) and his son King Mahipal (c. 912–940 CE) of the Gurjar–Pratihar dynasty whose capital was Kannauj. It was one of the most powerful kingdoms of the time whose sway extended from the Arabian Sea in the west to the borders of present day Bengal.

Rajshekhar wrote drama, poetry and literary theory. His well-known plays are *Balramayan*, *Balbharat*, *Viddhashalabhanjika* and *Karpuramanjari*. It is interesting to note that *Karpuramanjari* is not completely in Sanskrit. A major part is written in the Sauraseni Prakrit language. It is said that he wrote the play to please his wife Avantisundari, a woman of great literary taste. Rajshekhar is perhaps the only ancient Indian writer to mention his wife in his work and acknowledge her contribution to his literary career. In a poetic and loving manner, he describes her as 'chauhaanakulamaṇimaalaa' ('the gem-studded garland of the Chauhan clan').

Rajshekhar's *Kavyamimansa* is his only work on poetics. It is a wide-ranging work and the author's treatment of the subject is mature. Its eighteen chapters deal with subjects that include a history of Indian poetics, types of shaastraas, characteristic features of poetry, the qualities necessary for a poet and the kind of life he should lead, causes of poetic creation, forms of poetry, different types of sentences and rasa. His advice to aspiring poets is so detailed that it can be read as a handbook for poets.

Rajshekhar's defence of poetry is one of the highlights of *Kavyamimansa*. He shows how poetry is an extremely important subject which everyone must study. He first presents the arguments against poetry and then counters them. He says that critics of poetry contend that it should not be read because it is full of lies. Furthermore, its detractors also say that poetry is generally vulgar and leads people astray. Replying to these charges, Rajshekhar says that poetry only appears to be untrue but it is not so. In reality, it is nothing but the truth. It has a special way of describing things and this method of description can be seen in scriptures, scientific treatises as well as the daily conversation of people. He quotes stanzas from various scriptures and also from books on grammar to prove his point.

To support his contention that other subjects also use the same method of expression as poetry, he quotes a stanza from an ancient authority on grammar. The quoted stanza says that water is pure but maNtras are purer than water. The first three Vedas—*Rik*, *Yajur* and *Sama*—are purer than maNtras but grammar is the purest of them all. Rajshekhar says that this statement is clearly an exaggeration. One can find the same kind of exaggeration in poetry too but that does not make it untrue, just as the quoted hyperbolic statement does not make grammar untrue.

He also rejects the charge that poetry misguides people and promotes vulgarity. He points out that one should not go by the surface meaning of a verse but pay attention to what the intention of the poet is. The poet's intention is never to mislead people or to promote vulgarity. He defends poetry on the ground that it is necessary for life and provides joy to the reader. The arguments presented by him in defence of poetry remind us of those put forward by European poets and scholars such as Sir Philip Sidney and P.B. Shelley who also tried to defend poetry against the charge that it is not true or that it has no utility. In the Western tradition, this criticism that poets imitate the world and therefore are far removed from truth, as well as the charge they corrupt youth and incite passions instead of the faculty of reason, goes back to Plato. During Rajshekhar's time as well, similar charges were levelled against poetry to which he replied very ably.

Rajanak Kuntak

Rajanak Kuntak was a native of modern day Kashmir who lived in the latter half of the tenth century and was a contemporary of Rajshekhar. Kuntak focuses on poetic expression and establishes the centrality of language in poetry in his theory of poetics. He says that the function of language is different in poetry than in other situations. In poetry, language is essentially metaphorical and suggestive. One can say that he was one of the earliest language theorists in the subcontinent. The theory of poetry which he propagated is known as the theory of vakrokti and is laid down in his seminal text *Vakroktijeevit*. This book is divided into four chapters (unmeSh) in which the kaarikaas (memorial verses) and vrittis (explanation) are composed by Kuntak, while the examples have been taken from other writers.

In the first chapter of the book, Kuntak deals with kaavyaprayojan (the purpose of writing poetry) and kaavyalakShaṇ (characteristic features of poetry). Here he also introduces his concept of vakrokti and mentions its six types. By vakrokti he means an expression that is striking in its beauty and is markedly different from ordinary speech. He qualifies his statement by saying that every unusual expression is not vakrokti; it must be beautiful and should also be able to please the reader. He asserts that vakrokti is the defining feature (aatmaa or soul) of poetry. In the next three chapters of the book, Kuntak deals with different types of vakrokti.

Other scholars of the tenth century

There were a number of other scholars who lived in the same century as Rajshekhar and Kuntak. Mukul Bhatt belonged to modern day

Kashmir and lived in the first half of the tenth century. His only work is *Abhidhavrittimatrika* which is about shabdashakti or the different modes of signification that a word can have. The primary focus of the book is on abhidhaa (literal meaning) and lakShaṇaa (indicated sense). It is a short book with only fifteen kaarikaas and their explanations, but later scholars considered it a very important work, which is evident from the fact that Mammat used it as a source book for his treatment of shabdashakti.

Abhinavagupt lived in the second half of the tenth century and like many other scholars of poetics belonged to the modern day region of Kashmir Kashmir. He was a member of the court of King Lalitaditya of Kashmir. A prolific writer, he is said to have written some forty books of which *Abhinavbharati* and *Dhwanyaloklochan* deal with poetics. *Abhinavbharati* is a commentary on Bharat's *Natyashastra* and *Dhwanyaloklochan* is a detailed elucidation of Anandavardhan's *Dhwanyalok*. *Abhinavbharati* gives an exhaustive account of the theory of rasa and asserts that rasa is the essential element of poetry and that alaNkaars contribute to the generation of rasa. He adds that it is rasa which provides aanaNda or transcendental bliss to the reader. Abhinavagupt's *Dhwanyaloklochan*, a very important text of its time, is a lucid explication of the theory of dhwani.

Among other scholars of the tenth century are Rudrabhatt, Bhattalollat, Shrishankuk, Bhattataut and Dhananjay. The name of Rudrabhatt is often confused with that of Rudrat but they are different writers. Rudrabhatt came after Rudrat and wrote *Shringaratilak*, a work devoted primarily to a discussion of rasa while Rudrat belonged to the AlaNkaar School. Rudrabhatt rejects the view that there are ten rasas and claims that there are only nine. Bhattalollat, Shrishankuk and Bhattataut wrote very perceptive commentaries on Bharat's *Natyashastra* and are known primarily for their discussion of the theory of rasa. Dhananjay wrote *Dasharupakam* which many think is one of the most important texts on dramaturgy after *Natyashastra*. Like the other scholars mentioned here, he too was a follower of the Rasa School and was opposed to Anandavardhan's view that dhwani is the essence of poetry.

Kshemendra

The name of Kshemendra is associated with the theory of auchitya. Like Kuntak, he also belonged to the modern day region of Kashmir and lived in the eleventh century. He is supposed to have written over thirty books of which *Kavikanthabharan*, *Suvrittatilak* and *Auchityavicharcharcha* are concerned with poetics. *Kavikanthabharan* is a short book offering advice to poets about the ways in which they can develop their skill in poetry. *Suvrittatilak* deals with different kinds of poetic metres. *Auchityavicharcharcha* mentions twenty-seven kinds of auchitya and declares that auchitya is the core element of poetry. Auchitya comes from the Sanskrit word 'uchit', which means 'proper and right'. Kshemendra believes that various elements in poetry must be related to one another in a proper manner. In the absence of this quality of auchitya or the correctness of the interrelationship between the parts of poetry, it becomes lifeless even if it has guṇas or alaNkaars. To explain his point Kshemendra says, if a woman wears her ornaments on the wrong parts of her body she will become an object of ridicule. Similarly, if a man is aggressive to a person who has come to him for protection, or shows compassion to his enemy, he will be seen as foolish and everyone will laugh at him. In the same manner, to write good poetry a poet must use the right elements in the right proportion and order. However, after him auchitya failed to develop as an independent tradition of literary analysis. Most scholars consider auchitya as one of the many defining features of poetry and not its core element.

Bhojdev

Not only scholars but even some kings wrote books on literary theory. One such king was Bhojdev of the Parmar dynasty. He ruled from c. 1010–1055 CE over a large area in Central India. His capital was Dharanagar (the modern town of Dhar) and at the peak of his power he controlled an area which extended from Chittor (in present day Rajasthan) in the north to the upper Konkan (in present day Maharashtra) in the south and from the river Sabarmati in the east to Vidisha in the west. He fought many wars and made considerable extensions to his kingdom.

A renowned warrior, Bhojdev was also a great patron of art, literature and sciences. He was a prolific writer who is said to have written over eighty books on grammar, poetics and astrology. He was also a poet of considerable merit. *Saraswatikanthabharan* and *Shringarprakash* are two of his most important books on poetics. *Saraswatikanthabharan* has five chapters in which the first deals with the guṇas and doShas of poetry. The second, third and fourth chapters are concerned with different kinds of alaNkaars. The last chapter discusses a number of subjects including rasa and the types of heroines in drama. His *Shringarprakash* is one of the longest texts on Sanskrit poetics in which there are thirty-six chapters which deal with almost all the topics in poetics. Bhojdev believed that shriNgaar rasa or the emotion of erotic/romantic love is the core emotion in poetry. His discussion of alaNkaars is also very exhaustive. He has described a large number of alaNkaars and has explained them with multiple examples.

Table 2.2: Scholars from Anandavardhan to Bhojdev

Scholar	Century	Works	Main contribution
Anandavardhan	9th cent. CE	*Dhwanyalok*	founder of the Dhwani School
Rajshekhar	10th cent. CE	*Kavyamimansa*	offers a defence of poetry
Rajanak Kuntak	10th cent. CE	*Vakroktijeevit*	founder of the Vakrokti School
Mukul Bhatt	10th cent. CE	*Abhidhavrittimatrika*	discusses shabdashakti
Abhinavagupt	10th cent. CE	*Abhinavbharati* *Dhwanyaloklochan*	elucidates the ideas of Bharat and Anandavardhan
Rudrabhatt	10th cent. CE	*Shringaratilak*	writes primarily on rasa
Dhananjay	10th cent. CE	*Dasharupakam*	writes on dramaturgy
Kshemendra	11th cent. CE	*Kavikanthabharan*, *Suvrittatilak*, *Auchityavicharcharcha*	founder of the Auchitya School
Bhojdev	11th cent. CE	*Saraswatikanthabharan*, *Shringarprakash*	belongs to the Rasa School

Mammat

Mammat, a great Kashmiri scholar, lived in the second half of the eleventh century. We do not know much about his life except that as a student he spent some time in Kashi (Varanasi in modern day Uttar Pradesh) and that he was a devout worshipper of Lord Shiva. His most famous work is *Kavyaprakash*, which was written in the second half of the eleventh century. It is a kind of compendium in which Mammat tries to summarise and encapsulate various views on poetry put forward by earlier scholars.

Kavyaprakash is one of the most important texts of Indian poetics. Its importance can be gleaned from the fact that over seventy commentaries have been written on it. It was also translated into English by Dr Ganganath Jha. The book is divided into ten chapters called ullaas and has one hundred and forty-two kaarikaas. The kaarikaas and vrittis have been written by Mammat while the examples have been drawn from other writers. Mammat discusses subjects such as the purpose, causes, types and forms of poetry and the process by which meaning is generated. He also deals with dhwani, rasa, the properties and defects of poetry and various kinds of alaNkaars.

Agni Purana

The *Agni Purana*, one of the eighteen major Puranas of Hinduism, is not a book on poetics but there are some chapters in it which discuss topics related to literature. The consensus is that this Purana was written over some centuries and the earliest parts were composed sometime in the seventh century CE. Some scholars, such as Ludo Rocher (1926–2016), a Belgian-American Sanskrit scholar, believe that some parts of this Purana were added as late as the seventeenth century. It is a kind of encyclopaedia covering a vast range of subjects including mythology, cosmology, rituals, politics, diplomacy, military science, taxation theories, water distribution methods, building public projects, education, medicine, trees and plants, geography, grammar and poetics, to name a few. It has even a travel guide to Mithila in Bihar. Ten chapters—from chapter 336 to 346—deal with poetics.

As a text on poetics, the *Agni Purana* can be seen as a book that restates and sometimes explains the major ideas of scholars such as Bharat, Bhamah, Dandin, Anandavardhan, Bhojdev and Mammat. It discusses a number of topics in poetics such as rasa, alaNkaar, the characteristics of poetry, types of poetry, types of heroes and heroines in drama, and so on. There is also a section on acting in the book.

Scholars between the Agni Purana and Panditraj Jagannath

The period between the *Agni Purana* and Panditraj Jagannath is chiefly the time when various theories propounded earlier were closely analysed and some kind of relationship between them was discovered and discussed. During this period of about five hundred years, a number of texts on poetics were written. *Vyaktivivek*, written by Mahim Bhatt in the eleventh century, is one such important text. Mahim Bhatt was a Kashmiri scholar known for his critique of the theory of dhwani. He proposed that the idea of vyaNjanaa or suggested meaning is nothing more than mere conjecture. He believed that what really matters in kaavya is the literal sense of the words used in it. For him, even rasa was a matter of conjecture (anumaan). Like most books of its kind, *Vyaktivivek* has three parts: kaarikaa, vritti and udaaharaṇ (example). Sagarnandi was another writer who lived in the same century. He wrote *Natakalakshanaratnakosh,* an important work on dramaturgy.

In the twelfth century there were other scholars like Rajanak Ruyyak, whose *Alankarsarvaswa* is devoted primarily to a discussion of alaNkaars. The title 'Rajanak' before his name tells us that he belonged to present day Kashmir as it was given by Kashmiri kings to noted scholars. Ruyyak belongs to the AlaNkaar School as does Shobhakar Mitra who also lived in the same century. Another scholar who lived in the same century was Hemchandra, a Jain, who wrote *Kavyanushasanam* which summarises the ideas of other scholars before him.

In the next century there was Jaydev who was associated with the AlaNkaar School. We should remember that this writer is different from the poet Jayadev who wrote *Geet Govindam*. Vidyadhar, belonging to the same century, was a follower of the Dhwani School. This tells us that in the same age different viewpoints coexisted.

Mahapatra Vishwanath, who lived in the fourteenth century, is the author of *Sahityadarpan* ('The mirror of poetry'), which is one of the most popular books on the subject. In *Sahityadarpan* there is a reference to Allauddin Khilji (c.1296–1316CE), the Sultan of Delhi, which indicates that Vishwanath lived around that time, or at least after it. He belonged to Odisha and besides being a scholar of poetics was also a well-known poet and dramatist who wrote both in Sanskrit and Prakrit. Vishwanath declared that rasa is the soul of poetry and gave his well-known definition of poetry: 'vaakyam rasaatmakam kaavyam' ('poetry is that sentence that has rasa'). *Sahityadarpan* has ten chapters which discuss subjects such as the features of poetry, the purpose of poetry, shabdashakti, rasa, dhwani, guṇas and features of an epic.

Appaya Dikshit of the modern day Tamil Nadu is one of the major scholars of the sixteenth century. He was an extremely prolific writer who is said to have written about a hundred books. It is said that on the request of Venkata I, the King of Vijayanagar, Appaya Dikshit wrote his *Kuvalayanand*, an important text on Indian poetics. He wrote two other books on poetics—*Chitramimansa* and *Vrittavartika*. *Kuvalayanand* presents a detailed account of alaNkaars which is also the subject of *Chitramimansa*. *Vrittavartika* discusses the abhidhaa and lakShaṇaa powers of a word.

Panditraj Jagannath and after

Panditraj Jagannath belonged to the present day region of Andhra Pradesh. Later, he became a part of Mughal Emperor Shahjahan's (1592–1666 CE) court. The emperor valued Jagannath's literary abilities so highly that he conferred on him the title of 'Panditraj'. Panditraj Jagannath wrote a number of books of which *Chitramimansakhandan* and *Rasgangadhar* deal with poetics. *Chitramimansakhandan* is a critique of Appaya Dikshit's *Chitramimansa* in which Jagannaath rejects some of Appaya Dikshit's ideas concerning alaNkaars.

Panditraj Jagannath's *Rasgangadhar* explains a number of principles discussed by earlier scholars. He deviates from Bhamah's definition of poetry in the sense that he takes only language (shabda), and not meaning (artha), as the constituent element of poetry. He says that poetry is that kind of language which can convey a beautiful meaning ('ramaneeyaarth'). For him, beautiful meaning and the aesthetic pleasure that poetry provides are the same. Discussing the factors which make someone a poet, he says that it is only talent and nothing else which gives a person the ability to write poetry. He does not deny the role of learning and practice but if a person does not have talent, he cannot become a good poet. In his *Rasgangadhar* he has used self-composed verses as examples to illustrate the literary principles he discusses. He has dealt with features of poetry, types of poetry, guṇas of poetry and the theory of dhwani and alaNkaar. *Rasgangadhar* is a mature and comprehensive text on poetics but unfortunately it remained incomplete because of the untimely death of the author.

After Panditraj Jagannath, a number of scholars such as Ashadhar Bhatt, Vishweshwar Pandit and Narsingh Kavi wrote important books on poetics. Ashadhar Bhatt's *Trivenika*, for example, deals with the theory of meaning and discusses the various ways in which language can be used in literature.

Table 2.3: Scholars from Mammat to Panditraj Jagannath

Scholar	Century	Major works	Contribution
Mammat	11th cent. CE	*Kavyaprakash*	presents a compendium of earlier viewpoints in a single text
Agni Purana	11th cent. CE	The *Agni Purana*	offers a summary of the major ideas in poetics
Mahim Bhatt	11th cent. CE	*Vyaktivivek*	an anti-dhwani scholar
Rajanak Ruyyak	12th cent. CE	*Alankarsarvaswa*	a scholar of the AlaNkaar School
Vishwanath	14th cent. CE	*Sahityadarpan*	belongs to the Rasa School
Appaya Dikshit	16th cent. CE	*Kuvalayanand, Chitramimansa, Vrittavartika*	writes primarily on alaNkaars and shabdashakti

(*Contd.*)

Table 2.3: (*Contd.*)

Scholar	Century	Major works	Contribution
Panditraj Jagannath	17th cent. CE	*Rasgangadhar, Chitramimansakhandan*	gives an extensive account of the major issues in poetics; leans towards the Rasa School

SCHOOLS OF INDIAN POETICS

In Indian poetics, the term sampradaay, which means 'sect', is used to describe a group of scholars who give primacy to one particular theory of literature over others. These sampradaays may also be called 'schools'. In the course of the evolution of poetics in India six such major 'schools' emerged.

The Rasa School

Bharat is regarded as the founder of the Rasa School. His *Natyashastra* is taken to be the foundational text for the theory of rasa. Rajshekhar believes that even before Bharat, scholars like Nandikeshwar had discussed the concept of rasa and had established it as the core element of poetry. The theory of rasa explains the process by which a spectator feels the stirring of emotion when they are watching a theatrical performance. We will learn more about rasa later.

After Bharat a number of scholars discussed his concept of rasa and accepted it as the core element or aatmaa of poetry. Bhattanayak, Lollat, Shrishankuk and Abhinavagupt are some of the early scholars of the Rasa School. Bhattanayak argued that rasa is the core element of poetry. Abhinavagupt in his *Abhinavbharati* countered arguments against the theory of rasa and proposed that rasa is the defining feature of poetry.

Later scholars such as Dhananjay, Bhojdev and Mahim Bhatt accepted rasa as the most important element in poetry. Dhananjay's *Dasharupakam* focuses on rasa in drama and can be called the second most important text on dramaturgy after Bharat's *Natyashastra*.

Bhojdev wrote two important books on literary theory: *Saraswatikanthabharan* and *Shringarprakash*. Besides other topics,

Saraswatikanthabharan also discusses rasa, giving it a central place in the theory of poetics. *Shringarprakash* is a much longer text which discusses the same topics in greater detail.

Between the eleventh and thirteenth centuries there were a number of scholars of the Rasa School. *Natyadarpana*, which is another important text of this school, was written in the middle of the twelfth century. This text was written jointly by Ramchandra and Gunachandra and discussesd rasa in the tradition of the earlier scholars of this school such as Bharat and Dhananjay. Its four sections offered a comprehensive discussion of drama, rasa and features of the metaphor. Sharadatanay, who lived in the middle of the thirteenth century, also discussed the theory of rasa in his *Bhavprakashan*. Later in the early part of the fourteenth century, Vishwanath wrote on rasa and considered it the most important element of poetry. In his *Sahityadarpan* he discussed the theory of rasa in an extremely broad context. However, he also called dhwani kaavya the uttam (finest) kind of poetry, but he did it in the wider context of rasa and did not consider dhwani as being separate from rasa.

The last important scholar belonging to the Rasa School is Roopgoswami who lived in the middle of the sixteenth century. He wrote important texts such as *Natakachandrika*, *Bhaktirasamritasindhu* and *Ujjwalanilamani*. Inspired by the idea of the Vaishnavite concept of the sentiment of maadhurya (sweetness), Roopgoswami in his *Bhaktirasamritasindhu* conceived of a new rasa which he called 'ujjwal bhakti rasa', or the 'bright sentiment of devotion'. He considers this rasa to be primary, all other rasas being mere variants of this. In the later part of the sixteenth century, Jeevgoswami wrote commentaries on the works of Roopgoswami. Kavi Karnapur and Madhusudan Saraswati also lived in the same century and wrote on rasa.

The AlaNkaar School

Followers of the AlaNkaar School believe that alaNkaars or poetic devices are the defining feature of poetry. In other words, according to them alaNkaar is the soul of poetry. Thus, they distinguish between literary language and ordinary speech and believe that poetry cannot be written in a language which does not have the trappings of a 'literary' style, that is, which does not have alaNkaars.

Bhamah, Dandin, Udbhat and Rudrat are the earliest scholars of this school. These scholars lived between the sixth and ninth centuries, a period which saw the predominance of this theory. Bhamah was the first scholar to discuss alaNkaars in a comprehensive manner. In his *Kavyalankar* he listed a large number of poetic devices and included vakrokti, which literally means oblique speech, among the most important alaNkaars. The idea that vakrokti is merely an alaNkaar was contested by Kuntak some four hundred years later when he founded the Vakrokti School and called vakrokti the very soul of poetry, with all other elements of poetry subordinate to it.

Another major name among the scholars of the AlaNkaar School is that of Dandin. A close successor of Bhamah, he wrote *Kavyadarsh* which is influenced by Bhamah's work. Like Bhamah, Dandin also placed great emphasis on alaNkaar and gave it a central place in his scheme of poetics. Some two hundred years later Udbhat, another major scholar of the school, appeared on the scene. His *Kavyalankarsangrah* shows the influence of both Bhamah and Dandin. His work is notable for its subtle analysis of the theories of literature. Rudrat, belonging to the same period, is another important name in the history of this school but while accepting the position of his predecessors that alaNkaar is the essence of poetry, he also says that rasa is important as well.

The study of alaNkaar remained the dominant approach in critical methodology almost till the sixteenth century but the main tenets of the school had been established by the time of Rudrat himself. What scholars after Rudrat did was to redefine some of the key terms, explain them in greater detail, and add new alaNkaars to the already existing list. Among these later scholars are Ruyyak of the twelfth century who wrote *Alankarsarvaswa* and his contemporaries Hemchandra (author of *Kavyanushasanam*) and Vagbhatt (author of *Vagbhattalankar*). In the thirteenth century we have Jayadev Piyushvarsh (author of *Chandralok*). In the sixteenth century, Appaya Dikshit was another important scholar of the AlaNkaar School whose *Kuvalayanand* is an important book on alaNkaars.

The period between the sixth and ninth centuries can be called the golden age of the AlaNkaar School. After that period, the theory of rasa propounded by Bharat became prominent once again and alaNkaars as the all-important element of poetry took a back seat. When Bhattalollat and Shrishankuk wrote their commentaries on Bharat's *Natyashastra* they helped make rasa theory the central reference point for all literary discussion. Another factor which contributed to the emergence of rasa and dhwani as the guiding principles of literature was that philosophy, and not style and language, increasingly became the basis of discussion in Sanskrit literary theory. A few years after Shrishankuk, Rudrabhatt wrote his *Shringaratilak* in which he discussed shriNgaar rasa, underlining the importance of rasa once again. Thus, by the time the Dhwani School of Anandavardhan became the central tradition in Indian poetics, rasa as a guiding principle had already re-established itself. As a result of all this, the stream of the AlaNkaar School became weaker.

The Reeti School

In the eighth century, Vaman in his *Kavyalankarsutra* propounded a central, all-inclusive literary theory which came to be known as the theory of reeti. This theory became the basis of the establishment of the Reeti School in Indian poetics. Reeti can be defined as a particular kind of poetic diction. By asserting that reeti is the central element in literature, Vaman added a new chapter to Sanskrit poetics. Before Vaman, Bhamah and Dandin had also mentioned reeti while discussing poetry, but it is to Vaman's credit that he established it as an independent theory of literature. He considers reeti to be the soul of poetry and has discussed its types and subtypes in the first section of his *Kavyalankarsutra*.

The Vakrokti School

Rajanak Kuntak's most important contribution is that he established the theory of vakrokti and asserted that it is the very soul of poetry. Before him Bhamah, Dandin, Rudrat and Vaman had discussed vakrokti but only as an alaNkaar. Kuntak raised vakrokti to the level of the central guiding principle of poetry. He propounded his theory of vakrokti as a counter to the Dhwani School which was well established by that time. Kuntak discussed almost all the elements of poetry in the wider context of vakrokti. For him, any utterance which is different from ordinary speech and is also beautiful and striking is vakrokti. In other words, he clearly distinguishes between literary expression and ordinary speech. He believes that poetry is another name for that oblique expression which is created by the genius of the poet, and that is the reason why it is striking (that is, it has chamatkaar).

The Dhwani School

The period between the middle of the ninth century and the middle of the eleventh century may be called the golden age of the Dhwani School. In the ninth century, Anandavardhan propounded his theory of dhwani. In essence, this theory tries to analyse the suggestive power of poetry. Inspired by the concept of sphota in Sanskrit grammar, Anandavardhan declares that dhwani, and not rasa, alaNkaar or reeti, is the soul of poetry. He suggests that beyond its literal meaning, poetry also has a suggested meaning (vyaNgyaarth) which is the cause of poetic beauty. According to him all other elements of poetry such as rasa, alaNkaar and reeti are subordinate to dhwani.

Between the eleventh and seventeenth centuries there were a few scholars who strengthened the theory of dhwani and gave it its final form. During this period, Mammat (the second half of the eleventh century), Hemchandra (the second half of the twelfth century), Vidyadhar (the end of the thirteenth century) and Panditraj Jagannath (mid-seventeenth century), appear to lean towards the Dhwani School. Although Mammat's *Kavyaprakash* discusses various other topics, the primary focus of the book is on dhwani. He declares rasa to be a type of dhwani and calls it 'rasadhwani'. Panditraj Jagannath was the last important scholar of the Dhwani School. In his *Rasgangadhar* he counters the views of earlier scholars such as Appaya Dikshit and others and establishes the centrality of dhwani in poetry. He, however, gives equal importance to rasa. In his classification of dhwani into five types he includes rasadhawani and calls it the most important element of poetry.

The Auchitya School

Kshemendra propounded the Auchitya School of poetics. His major works are *Auchityavicharcharcha* and *Kavikanthabharan*. As its title suggests, *Auchityavicharcharcha* deals with the element of auchitya in literature, its different types and subtypes, and declares that the element of auchitya (that is, harmony and consistency) is everything in poetry. However, the theory of auchitya could not gain the kind of salience other schools of poetics did.

This is just a brief glimpse of various scholars, their work and contribution as well as the prominent schools of Indian poetics. We read about Ruyyak, Jaydev, Appaya Dikshit belonging to the AlaNkaar School; Bharat who founded the Rasa School and Ramchandra, Gunachandra, Vishwanath, Shardatanay, Roopgoswami and others who contributed to it. There were also scholars like Mammat, Panditraj Jagannath, Hemchandra and Vidyadhar who strengthened the theory of dhwani and gave it its final form, along with Vaman of the Reeti School, Kuntak of the Vakrokti School and Kshemendra from the Auchitya School. Their works are wide and deep and are spread over centuries. A detailed discussion of these schools and theories will be seen in later chapters.

3

Aspects of Poetry

- Characteristic features of poetry (kaavyalakShaṇ)
- Causes of poetic creation (kaavyahetu)
- Purpose of poetry (kaavyaprayojan)
- Qualities of poetry (guṇas)
- Kinds of poetry (bhedas)

CHARACTERISTIC FEATURES OF POETRY (KAAVYALAKSHAṆ)

Since the time of Bharat, Indian scholars have been trying to identify the features or lakShaṇs of poetry. Bharat was the first to describe the features of a good play. Some eight centuries later, Bhamah became the first scholar to define poetry. His definition became the model for all the later definitions of poetry. When Bhamah defined poetry as a 'fusion of word and meaning' he was suggesting two things simultaneously: first, poetry is indeed a special kind of writing (or shabda) and secondly, it is not complete without its artha. Now, what is artha? It is the shabda's impact on the reader. Thus, from the very beginning our scholars considered the reader's response to poetry as an essential ingredient of poetry.

Bharat: Features of Poetry

Bharat in his *Natyashastra* mentions seven features of poetry. We should remember that he was discussing the features of poetry in the context of drama, which was called 'drishya kaavya' or 'poetry meant to be seen'. He writes:

> मृदुललितपदाढ्यं गूढशब्दार्थहीनं
> जनपदसुखबोध्यं युक्तिमन्नृत्ययोज्यम्।
> बहुकृतरसमार्गं संधिसंधानयुक्तं
> स भवति शुभकाव्यं नाटकप्रेक्षकाणाम्। (*नाट्यशास्त्र*)

> mridulalitpadaaDhyaM gooDhashabdaarthaheenaM
> janapadasukhabodhyaM yuktimannrityayojyam ।
> bahukritarasamaargaM saNdhisaNdhaanayuktaM
> sa bhavati shubhkaavyaM naatakaprekShakaaṇaaM । (*Natyashastra*)
>
> That kaavya is good for the spectators of drama which has been written in soft and beautiful language; in which words and their meaning are not obscure; which the common person can easily understand; which is logically sound (that is, which does not violate the conventions of good sense); which can form the basis of a dance performance; which can evoke multiple rasas and which is written in such a manner that there is no break in the flow of emotions.

These seven features highlight the basic requirements of a good play. The first requirement is that its language should sound pleasant. But this in itself is not enough; the language should also be intelligible to the spectator. Bharat thus shifts the focus from the writer of the play to its spectator. If a person watching a play has to make an effort to understand what is being said, they will not be able to enjoy it and consequently, no rasa will be generated. Rasa, as we shall see later, is a term used to describe the aesthetic flavour of a work of art (such as a play) that evokes an emotion in the sensitive reader or spectator (sahridaya). The rasas, which are nine in number, are created by bhaavs, or different states of mind. In the absence of rasa, the spectator will feel no aanaNd or aesthetic joy. If this happens, the play has failed to perform its primary function and therefore, is not a good play.

The third feature defines the spectator who is a common person and may not be highly educated. The play is meant for them and must please them. That is the reason why Bharat uses the expression 'janapadasukhabodhyaM'. 'Janapada' means a 'community of common, ordinary people'. To be called successful, the play must be comfortably ('sukh') understood ('bodhyaM') by the common spectator.

The next two features are related to the content of the play. Bharat says that a play is good only if the story it depicts is logically sound and does not offend our common sense. The fifth feature is related to the presentation of the play. Dance and music were common features of ancient Sanskrit drama and that is why Bharat wants its language to be such that it can be set to music and be used in a dance performance.

The last two features of drama are again related to the spectator. Bharat says that a good play should allow the spectator to taste rasa, which means that it should evoke emotions in the spectator. And finally, he says that a good play is written in such a way that there is no break in the flow of emotions. The seventh condition is a prerequisite for the fulfilment of the sixth because if there is a break in the flow of emotions, the spectator cannot experience rasa. We shall see how rasa is a unified and ceaseless experience in Chapter 5.

Post-Bharat Scholars: Features of Poetry

Bharat's definition of a good play is fairly comprehensive and covers major aspects such as language, content and its emotional impact on the spectator. As mentioned earlier, Bhamah was the first scholar to define poetry as a conjugation of word (shabda) and meaning (artha).

What does Bhamah mean by shabda (word) and artha (meaning)? Why does he say that poetry is possible only when shabda and artha combine? Defining something like poetry is extremely difficult because it can mean different things to different people. According to the conditions specified by scholars of the Nyaay School of Hindu philosophy, for a definition to be sound, it must not suffer from three kinds of flaws: ativyaapti (over extension), avyaapti (non-extension) and asambhav (impossibility). 'Ativyaapti' means that the definition must not cover such a vast area so as to become meaningless. 'Avyaapti' means that it should not leave out some essential feature. And 'asambhav' means that it should not include a feature that is impossible. If we apply this yardstick to Bhamah's definition, it seems to suffer from the fault of ativyaapti or over extension because every single utterance is a combination of word and meaning. Then how does this definition help us differentiate between poetry and non-poetry?

To answer this question, we should understand the context in which Bhamah gives this definition. Before defining poetry, he discusses the views of scholars who came before him. He says that while some of them give importance only to shabdaalaNkaars (figures of speech related to words) others have emphasised only arthaalaNkaars, or figures of speech related to meaning. Then he says that it is his view that the union of both shabdaalaNkaars and arthaalaNkaars is necessary for poetry. It is implicit in this definition that Bhamah considers alaNkaars, or poetic devices, to be a characteristic feature of poetry.

We see that Bhamah's definition covers both the reading and the writing of poetry. Shabda denotes writing. He suggests that poetry is indeed a special kind of shabda, or language, but that is only one part of it. The shabda needs to be recognised as poetry by the reader—that is, the reader should imbue the shabda with the artha (meaning) it needs to be given. Again, unlike other kinds of writing, the meaning of poetry is not limited to understanding the thoughts and ideas of the writer. It also includes the emotions we experience while reading a poem. Since poetry tries to communicate experience, the emotions we experience while reading a poem are also a part of its artha or meaning. This aspect of the artha of poetry is difficult to describe and that is probably one of the reasons why it is difficult to define poetry in a manner that will satisfy everyone.

Bhamah's definition of poetry is important because it became the common reference point for later scholars. Most scholars after Bhamah accept poetry as a 'word-meaning combine' but they differ in their emphasis of its other features. Some assert that guṇas (qualities of poetry) are the essential features of poetry. Others think that it is alaNkaar that is the core feature, while some others take rasa to be the central feature of poetry. Because of this difference of opinion, we have different schools in Indian poetics. Followers of a particular school consider a specific element of poetry to be its aatmaa (soul).

After Bhamah, it was Dandin in the seventh century who accepted the definition that poetry is a combination of shabda and artha but he also added that alaNkaars are an essential part of it. Dandin was one of the earliest scholars of the AlaNkaar School and therefore it was difficult for him to accept that there can be any poetry without poetic devices. In the next century, Vaman concurred with Bhamah and said that poetry is indeed the fusion of language and meaning, but also added that guṇa is the basic feature of poetry. He claimed that the use of alaNkaars was optional. Vaman also mentions the absence of doShas or flaws as being another feature of poetry.

In the ninth century, Udbhat wrote about the characteristic features of poetry and accepted Bhamah's definition that poetry is a combination of word and meaning, and added that to be beautiful, it should be flawless. He considered guṇas to be the central feature of poetry. AlaNkaars are welcome but they are not compulsory, although if used, they add to the beauty of a poetic composition. Thus, Udbhat follows Vaman in saying that alaNkaars are optional in poetry.

From this brief summation of the characteristic features of poetry as described by scholars between the sixth and ninth centuries, it is obvious that there is very little difference in the definitions of poetry given by Bhamah, Dandin, Vaman and Udbhat. What was added to Bhamah's definition was that poetry should also have guṇas, alaNkaars and should be free from doShas. Not all these scholars, however, felt that alaNkaars are absolutely essential to poetry.

After them, Kuntak says poetry is that strikingly beautiful composition in which words and meaning are organised according to a particular order, and which gives aesthetic pleasure to the reader. He too calls poetry a conjugation of shabda and artha but his emphasis is on the striking quality (vakrataa) of poetry. By vakrataa he means that quality in the composition which separates it from ordinary speech. Thus, poetry is essentially a baNdha or composition in which this vakrataa is revealed. And finally, this vakrataa in the composition should be able to give aesthetic pleasure to the reader. It is clear that Kuntak distinguishes between poetic diction and ordinary speech and considers vakrokti or poetic diction to be the basic feature of poetry.

In the eleventh century while discussing the characteristic features of poetry, both Bhojdev and Mammat followed their predecessors, but they also emphasised some other elements in it. Highlighting the element of rasa in poetry, Bhojdev says that a composition which can evoke rasa is poetry. He thus includes the capacity to evoke rasa as among the basic features of poetry. Rasa, as we shall see later, is a term used to describe the aesthetic flavour of a work of art (such as a play) that evokes an emotion in the sensitive reader or spectator (sahridaya). The rasas, which are nine in number, are created by bhaavs or the different states of mind. He also says that the language of poetry should be embellished with alaNkaars, contain the guṇas of poetry and be free from doShas.

In the same century, Mammat, the author of *Kayvaprakash*, also discussed the characteristic features of poetry. Like Bhojdev, he also says that poetry is that shabdaarth (word–meaning combine) which has the guṇas of poetry and is free from flaws. He, however, differs from Bhojdev when he says that poetry is possible even without using alaNkaars. He writes:

> तददोषौ शब्दार्थौ सगुणावनलंकृती पुनः क्वापि। (*काव्यप्रकाश*)
>
> tadadoShau shabdaarthau saguṇaavanalaNkriti punah kvaapi ।
> (*Kavyaprakash*)
>
> Those words and their meanings which are free from defects, have guṇas, and which at times can also be without alaNkaars, are called poetry.

Mammat's definition of poetry continued to guide later scholars when they sought to describe the characteristic features of poetry. For example, Hemchandra, a twelfth century scholar of poetics, writes in his *Kavyanushasanam*:

> अदोषौ सगुणौ सालंकारौ शब्दार्थौ काव्यम्। (*काव्यनुशासनम्*)
>
> adoShau saguṇau saalaNkaarau shabdaarthau kaavyam ।
> (*Kavyanushasanam*)
>
> Poetry is that word–meaning combine which is free from defects, has the guṇas of poetry and is embellished with alaNkaars.

As we can see, Hemchandra's definition is not very different from that given by earlier scholars.

In the fourteenth century, Vishwanath criticised Mammat's definition of poetry on three counts. First, he objects to the inclusion of 'freedom from flaws' (adoShau) in the definition on the grounds that even the finest poetry may have some flaws, but we do not call it non-poetry simply because of that. Thus, adoShau is a negative attribute of poetry and should not be mentioned among its features. Secondly, if, according to Mammat, alaNkaar is not an essential element of poetry it should not have been mentioned at all. A definition of something cannot have elements that are only occasionally present in it. And finally, Vishwanath complains that in his definition, Mammat mentions only guṇas and not rasa, dhwani or vakrokti and therefore it is an incomplete definition. After highlighting the weaknesses in Mammat's definition of poetry, Vishwanath offers his own:

> वाक्यं रसात्मकं काव्यम्। (*साहित्यदर्पण*)
>
> vaakyaM rasaatmakaM kaavyaM | (*Sahityadarpaṇ*)
>
> The sentence which has rasa is poetry.

Here he is closer to Bhojdev because the latter also established the centrality of rasa in poetry. When rasa is taken as the essential element of poetry, all other elements are naturally included because these elements are necessary for the generation of rasa.

In the seventeenth century, Panditraj Jagannath deviated from Bhamah's definition in a very important sense. Jagannath asserted that poetry is not a combination of language and meaning as claimed by Bhamah but is primarily and solely language which conveys a beautiful meaning. For 'beautiful' he uses the word 'ramaṇeeya'. It is an adjective that suggests a thing that is lovely and delightful. If a composition looks beautiful to the reader and also pleases them, it is poetry. He writes:

> रमणीयार्थप्रतिपादकः शब्दः काव्यम्। (*रसगंगाधर*)
>
> ramaṇeeyaarthapratipaadakah shabdah kaavyaM | (*Rasgangadhar*)
>
> Poetry is that word which gives a beautiful meaning.

Thus, poetry for Jagannaath is primarily that shabda which is able to please the reader because of its capacity to convey a beautiful meaning. We should note that here the word 'beautiful' has been used in its widest sense. Writing to which one returns again and again, because each time it is read it conveys something new and therefore something beautiful, is poetry.

Table 3.1: Characteristic features of poetry

Scholar	Century	Characteristic features
Bharat	2nd cent. BCE	(*Described in the context of drama*) mellifluous; intelligible; accessible to common people; logically sound; fit to be used in a dance performance; having the capacity to evoke rasa and able to give ceaseless aesthetic experience
Bhamah	6th cent. CE	a combination of shabda and artha
Dandin	7th cent. CE	a combination of shabda and artha embellished with alaNkaars
Vaman	8th cent. CE	a combination of shabda and artha with guṇas and alaNkaars
Udbhat	8th cent. CE	a combination of shabda and artha, with guṇas, alaNkaars and without defects
Kuntak	10th cent. CE	vakra (beautiful and inspired) composition giving pleasure to the reader
Bhojdev	11th cent. CE	capable of evoking rasa; having alaNkaars and guṇas and without defects
Mammat	11th cent. CE	a combination of shabda and artha, without defects, with guṇas and occasionally without alaNkaars
Hemchandra	12th cent. CE	a combination of shabda and artha, with guṇas, alaNkaars and free from defects
Vishwanath	14th cent. CE	a combination of shabda and arthaevoking rasa
Panditraj Jagannath	17th cent. CE	shabda that conveys beautiful meaning

The Aatmaa (Soul) of Poetry

Over the centuries, scholars have debated what is the core feature or the aatmaa of poetry. They have described poetry as having a body (the language) and a soul (its essence). Vaman was the first to mention the soul of poetry. Since he belonged to the Reeti School, he identified reeti as the soul of poetry. He says, 'vishiShTapadarachanaa reetih' ('reeti is a special arrangement of padas'). By 'vishiShTapadarachana' he means an expression which has the guṇas of poetry. Thus, for him the particular form in which poetry is written is its soul or defining feature.

The followers of the Rasa School declared that rasa is the soul of poetry. In Chapter Three of his *Kavyamimansa*, Rajshekar says that if a piece of writing can evoke emotions (rasa) in a reader, it is poetry. The language in which it is written is its body and its ability to evoke emotion is its soul. Abhinavagupt also agrees with Rajshekhar and considers rasa to be the soul of poetry while alaNkaars are its ornaments. Kuntak considers vakrokti the soul of poetry. By this he meant that poetry is defined by its obliqueness of expression. We shall learn more about reeti, rasa and vakrokti in later chapters.

CAUSES OF POETIC CREATION (KAAVYAHETU)

The qualities a person should possess in order to write poetry is the subject of kaavyahetu. 'Hetu' means cause or reason, so kaavyahetu means those factors or conditions which are responsible for the writing of poetry. Scholars have identified many factors which help a person write poetry but all of them agree that there are three fundamental qualities one must possess in order to write poetry: talent, training and practice.

Bhamah says that the first thing a person needs to write poetry is talent. Then he goes on to say that someone wishing to write poetry must also have an exceptional command over language but adds that without talent this ability is of no use. A poet must also have a very good education, and they should have learnt the craft of poetry from other poets.

Dandin's views about kaavyahetu are slightly different. He also accepts the three primary causes of poetry—talent, knowledge of literature and continuous practice of the craft—but believed that a person may become a poet through a combination of study and practice, even if they are not talented. Vaman does not accept this and believes that talent is essential for a poet. Anandavardhan and Abhinavagupt also consider talent to be the primary cause of poetry.

In his *Kavyamimansa*, Rajshekhar discusses in detail the factors which cause poetry to be written. He says that while training and practice are important, what really matters in a poet is their natural gift for writing poetry. The implication is that talent is something that cannot be taught. For talent, he uses two terms, 'shakti' and 'pratibhaa', and goes on to distinguish between them. Shakti is the natural ability a person is born with while pratibhaa is that power in a poet which lights up the words they use. We can also say that shakti is a person's intelligence, energy and originality of thinking, while pratibhaa is their creative imagination. Rajshekhar says that a poet who has pratibhaa can see with their mind's eye even that which is not present before them, while a person without pratibhaa cannot see anything beyond what is present before them. He then identifies two kinds of pratibhaa: kaaryitri and bhaavyitri. Poets have kaaryitri pratibhaa. It means that they can create poetry. Critics have bhaavyitri pratibhaa which gives them the ability to understand poetry.

Kuntak, Mammat and Panditraj Jagannath also consider talent or shakti to be the primary cause of poetry. Besides talent, Kuntak mentions vyutpatti (learning) and abhyaas (practice) as necessary qualities for a poet. Mammat echoes Kuntak, the difference being that for vyutpatti he has used the term nipuṇataa, which, according to him, is the expertise a poet acquires when he observes life closely and reads texts on various subjects (including literature). Mammat, however, does not say that any one of these three qualities is more important than others. He believes that all these three must be present simultaneously for poetry to be written. He says:

> शक्तिर्निपुणता लोकशास्त्राद्यवेक्षणात्,
> काव्यज्ञशिक्षयाभ्यास इतिहेतुस्तदुद्भवे। (*काव्यप्रकाश*)
>
> shaktirnipuṇataa lokashaastraadyavekShaṇaat,
> kaavyagyashikShayaabhyaas itihetustadudbhave । (*Kavyaprakash*)
>
> Talent for writing poetry (shakti), expertise gained by observing society, studying the shastras and poetry etc., gaining knowledge

from poets and critics (nipuṇataa) and then practising the art (abhyaas)—a combination of all these three things cause the birth of poetry.

The writing of poetry has often been explained with the help of an analogy. A poet is like a potter. A potter needs clay, a wheel and the stick to turn it with in order to make earthen pots. He needs all these three things at the same time. In the same manner, a poet needs to have talent, knowledge and continuous practice at the same time in order to write poems.

Panditraj Jagannath however, believes that talent is the only cause of poetry. Sometimes this talent expresses itself naturally and sometimes the poet's education and practice of the art help reveal it. Jagannaath says that there are poets who begin writing poetry at a very early age, sometimes even before completing their education. Later, they develop their art with practice. This happens because they have talent to begin with. Jagannath therefore believes that no matter how highly educated a person is or how hard they have worked, they will never be a poet if they lack a natural gift for writing poetry.

Table 3.2: Causes of poetic creation (kaavyahetu)

Scholar	Period	Causes of poetry/the qualities needed in a poet
Bhamah	6th cent. CE	talent, a mastery over language, learning from literature and other poets
Dandin	7th cent. CE	talent, knowledge of literature and continuous practice
Vaman	8th cent. CE	talent, knowledge of literature and continuous practice
Anandavardhan	9th cent. CE	primarily talent, but education and training are important
Rajshekhar	10th cent. CE	talent and creative imagination
Mammat	11th cent. CE	shakti (talent), nipuṇataa (education) and abhyaas (practice)
Panditraj Jagannath	17th cent. CE	primarily talent—sometimes unschooled and sometimes developed by practice

THE PURPOSE OF POETRY (KAAVYAPRAYOJAN)

Kaavyaprayojan means the purpose for which poetry is written or read. Scholars who discuss the purpose of poetry believe that literature plays a very important role in a person's life. Bharat was the first to write about the purpose of poetry:

> धर्म्यम् यशस्य आयुष्यम् हितं बुद्धिविवर्द्धनम्,
> लोकोपदेशजननं नाट्यमेतद् भविष्यति। (*नाट्यशास्त्र*)
>
> dharmyaM yashasya aayuShyaM hitaM buddhivivardhanam,
> lokopadeShjananaM naatyametad bhaviShyati । (*Natyashastra*)
>
> Drama is a means of acquiring virtue, gaining fame, enjoying longevity, being blessed, sharpening the intellect and providing instruction to the people.

These six benefits include physical (longevity), intellectual (getting an education and sharpening the intellect), spiritual (becoming virtuous and receiving the blessings of the Almighty) and social (becoming famous) benefits. It is a fairly comprehensive list of the good effects of poetry.

While mentioning the different purposes of reading and writing poetry in his *Kavyalankar*, Bhamah underlines its multiple advantages:

> धर्मार्थकाममोक्षेषु वैचक्षण्यं कलासु च,
> करोति कीर्तिं प्रीतिं च साधुकाव्यनिबन्धनम्।
>
> dharmaarthakaammokSheShu vaichakShaṇyaM kalaasu cha,
> karoti keertiM preetiM cha saadhukaavyanibandhanam ।
>
> Good poetry helps a person to achieve the four objectives of life, which are dharma (virtue), artha (wealth), kaama (desire) and mokSh (salvation). It gives him expertise in every art. He gains fame by it. He experiences joy and gives delight to others.

It is clear from this verse that for Bhamah, the writing and reading of poetry is one of the most important activities in life. He establishes a relationship between poetry and the four fundamental puruShaarthas (objectives) of life as specified by Hinduism. According to Hindu philosophy, every person has to achieve four things in life without which they cannot be called successful—these are dharma, artha, kaama and mokSh. 'Dharma' stands for virtue, duty and moral values. Bhamah suggests that poetry can help morally uplift a person. 'Artha' means gaining material wealth; one of the primary purposes of writing and reading poetry is to achieve prosperity. It is not too difficult to understand the link between poetry and prosperity if we realise that in Bhamah's time, a person who wrote (or even read) poetry was considered very highly educated and was part of the social elite. 'Kaama' can be translated as desire, pleasure, love and other positive psychological states. When prosperity is achieved, desires can also be fulfilled. 'MokSh' means salvation and spiritual growth. He believes that poetry also plays a role in the religious and spiritual life of a person. Apart from helping a person to achieve these four aims of life, poetry also makes them proficient in different arts. It gives them fame and the love of many.

Vaman mentions only two primary purposes of poetry which are 'driShT' (which can be seen) and 'adriShT' (which cannot be seen). Preeti (joy or delight) is the visible purpose of writing poetry while keerti or fame is that which cannot be seen. He writes:

> काव्यं सद् दृष्टादृष्टार्थं प्रीतिकीर्तिहेतुत्वात्। (*काव्यालंकारसूत्र*)
>
> kaavyam sad driShTaadriShTaartham preetikeertihetutwaat |
> (*Kavyalankarsutra*)
>
> True poetry has a visible and invisible purpose; preeti is the visible purpose and keerti is the purpose that is not visible.

Commentators have defined preeti as the delight experienced by the reader while reading poetry. Anandavardhan and Abhinavagupt also mention preeti as a purpose of poetry and define it as aesthetic delight. Keerti has been described as a means by which the poet ascends to heaven which is why it has been called the 'unseen' purpose of poetry. But keerti can also be interpreted as fame which continues even after the poet's death and in this sense, it is something which the poet cannot see in his lifetime.

Rudrat mentions six purposes of poetry. First, a poet's work brings them fame; second, it brings fame to the hero of their poem; third, the poet gains wealth; fourth, when their poetry praises the gods they become free from illness; fifth, they get whatever they desire in life, and sixth, they achieve the four aims of life, that is, dharma, artha, kaama and mokSh. The first five benefits are for the poet while the last is for both the poet and the reader.

After Rudrat, Kuntak wrote about the purpose of poetry. According to him the primary purpose of poetry is antashchamatkaar or spiritual expansion of the poet and the reader.

The different purposes of writing and reading poetry were again mentioned by Mammat in the eleventh century. These benefits cover multiple aspects of life: material, social, moral, emotional and intellectual. In the opening chapter of *Kavyaprakash* he writes:

> काव्यम् यशसे अर्थकृते व्यवहारविदे शिवेतरक्षतये,
> सद्यः परनिर्वृत्तये कान्तासम्मिततयोपदेश युजे।
>
> kaavyam yashase arthkrite vyavahaaravide shivetarakShataye,
> sadyah paranirvrittaye kaantaasammitatayopadesha yuje ।
>
> Poetry is for gaining fame, acquiring wealth, learning proper social behaviour, destroying evil in a person, feeling instantaneous joy and being educated in a pleasing manner: the manner in which a beloved teaches her man.

These six purposes of poetry suggest that the principle of 'art for art's sake' was not accepted, nor was literature judged only on the basis of its 'practical' utility. Mammat mentions fame as the first purpose of poetry probably because the respect that a poet gets is paramount. That is the reason why yash or fame is mentioned first. Secondly, poetry is also mentioned as being a prosperous profession as most poets had wealthy patrons, such as kings and royal families. Mammat must have been writing from his own experience. Thirdly, poetry performs a social function of 'vyavahaaravide' or 'that which is used to learn the proper code of social conduct'. It is a function which history cannot perform. The fourth purpose of poetry is 'shivetarakShataye' or 'for the destruction of evil'. 'Shiva' means 'good' and 'shivetar' refers to everything that is the opposite of 'good' ('itar' means 'beyond', or the 'opposite of'). Thus, poetry performs a moral function as it destroys evil in its writer and reader. The fifth purpose of poetry is that it provides immediate (sadyah) pleasure. This applies to both the poet and the reader. And finally, he says that poetry also teaches us in a very gentle and sweet manner, in the same way a beloved or wife (kaanta) does ('kaantaasammitatayopadesha yuje').

Mammat is building on one of the three kinds of teaching methods recognised in ancient India: prabhusammit, mitrasammit and kaantaasammit. Prabhusammit is a teaching method in which a disciple is instructed about what can and cannot be done. In this case, the teacher is seen as someone who cannot be disobeyed. The Vedas have been seen as one such prabhu or master who can never be disobeyed. For example, when the Vedas command, 'Speak the truth', or when they order, 'Follow dharma' (that is, 'do your duty') they cannot be challenged and have to be obeyed at all times. Then, there is mitrasammit—teaching in the manner of a mitra or friend. What we learn from history is an example of mitrasammit teaching. We can question the veracity of that knowledge and can also reject it in the same manner as we sometimes disagree with our friend. And finally, there is another kind of teaching called kaantaasammit. What we learn from poetry is kaantaasammit because the process of learning is pleasant. As a beloved (kaanta) can change the behaviour of the lover without their realising it, thus can poetry also teach us in a gentle manner. Horace says in his *Ars Poetica*, 'To teach, to please, these are the poet's aims, or at once to profit and to amuse'. And Sir Philip Sidney in his *An Apology for Poetry* writes, 'The poet does not merely show the way, but giveth so sweet a prospect into the way, as will entice any man to enter into it'.

These six kaavyaprayojan do not concern only the poet. While gaining fame and wealth are related exclusively to the poet, learning proper social behaviour, receiving immediate pleasure and gaining knowledge in a pleasant manner are concerned with the reader. Destruction of evil is related both to the poet and the reader.

Table 3.3: The purpose of poetry

Scholar	Purpose
Bharat	to become virtuous, gain fame, enjoy a long life, receive divine blessings, become more intelligent and learn new things
Bhamah	to achieve the four aims of life, gain expertise in every art, become famous and get pleasure
Vaman	for preeti (both to the poet and the reader) and keerti
Rudrat	to become famous, make one's hero famous, gain wealth, become free from illness, have one's desires fulfilled and achieve the four aims of life
Mammat	to become famous, prosperous, learn proper social behaviour, become free from evil, receive immediate pleasure and learn in a pleasant manner

THE QUALITIES (GUṆAS) OF POETRY

'Guṇa' in Sanskrit means the 'property of something'. For example, it is the guṇa of water to flow and the guṇa of fire to burn. In poetics, guṇas mean qualities associated with poetry. Like a person who possesses qualities of virtue, compassion, courage and generosity is respected, poetry which has guṇas such as maadhurya, oja and prasaad is considered beautiful.

A number of scholars have discussed the nature and number of kaavyaguṇas, or qualities of poetry. Fundamentally, these qualities are related to the manner in which a person uses language. In Jain literature, for example, we come across thirty-five adjectives for the different qualities of language. Kautilya's *Arthashastra* talks about the defining features of language that is used for writing. We read about the udaar (generous) and madhur (sweet) guṇas of speech in the Ramayana. The Mahabharata also mentions qualities of speech such as paruSh (harsh) and madhur (sweet). Kalidas's works also explore shleSh, prasaad, maadhurya and oja guṇas as the characteristic features of different kinds of speech.

Bharat was the first scholar to define the guṇas of poetry. He describes guṇas as the absence of doShas (defects), where doShas are those elements which diminish the beauty of poetry. Bharat mentions ten guṇas of poetry: shleSh, prasaad, samataa, samaadhi, maadhurya, oja, pada-saukumaarya, arthavyakti, udaarataa, udaattataa and kaanti. ShleSh means a style of writing using words which have coalesced or been joined through meaning. Prasaad refers to a style in which there is an easy flow of the verse. Samataa indicates consistency in style. Samaadhi is the rhythmic rise and fall of verse. That sweetness which is a result of using short words is maadhurya. The use of long and compound words conveying a feeling of strength and energy is the oja guṇa. The absence of harshness in style is pada-saukumaarya. Expressing meaning clearly is arthavyakti. Richness in expression is udaarataa. Udaattataa is the quality of exaltedness of style and kaanti is that loveliness which is born out of the novelty and freshness of expression. These are the qualities good poetry must have.

After Bharat, Bhamah discussed the guṇas of poetry in his *Kavyalankar*. He does not accept the ten guṇas mentioned by Bharat and instead says that there are only three guṇas: maadhurya, oja and prasaad. He feels all the other guṇas mentioned by Bharat are covered by these three.

Vaman mentions ten guṇas and says that both guṇas and alaNkaars play an equal part in generating rasa. Many of the guṇ as he mentions are the same as those named by Bharat. According to Vaman the ten guṇas of poetry are the following: shleSh (when phrases appear to be flowing as one), samataa (consistency; when the verse or poem begins and ends in the same style), samaadhi (the rise and fall of the rhythm in the verse), maadhurya (sweetness resulting from the use of short phrases), saukumaarya (the tenderness of verse where something harsh is being said in a mild manner), udaarataa (when the reader feels that the phrases are dancing and there is a lack of roughness and crudity about them), arthavyakti (immediately intelligible), and kaanti (the presence of beauty in a line).

Later scholars such as Abhinavagupt, Anandavardhan and Mammat accepted only maadhurya, oja and prasaad as guṇas of poetry. Anandavardhan says in his *Dhwanyalok* that guṇas like maadhurya are the properties of rasa which is the soul of poetry and not a feature of words or word order. Following Anandavardhan, Mammat also says that guṇas are the properties of rasa and not of language. He illustrates his point by saying that as courage is the property of the soul and not of the body, guṇa is the dharma (the basic property) of rasa (the soul of poetry), and not that of language (the body of poetry). In his *Kavyaprakash*, Mammat discusses the nature and number of guṇas. Defining guṇa he says:

> ये रसस्याङ्गिनो धर्माः शौर्यादय इवात्मनः,
> उत्कर्षहेतवस्तेस्युरचलस्थितयो गुणाः ।
>
> ye rasasyaaNgino dharmaah shauryaadaya ivaatmanah,
> utkarShahetavastesyurachalasthitayo guṇaah ।
>
> As courage and similar other qualities are the properties of the soul, guṇas are the properties of rasa, which themselves are the soul of poetry. Guṇas are always found with rasas and are a means of their intensification.

Therefore, he says, guṇas always appear in conjugation with rasas. What Mammat is saying here is that if there is a particular guṇa (a specific structure and sound of the verse resulting in a particular effect) in a piece of poetry, a specific set of emotions will be aroused and a particular rasa will be generated in the reader.

Before we discuss the nature of the three guṇas—maadhurya, oja and prasaad—we need to understand the three different states of mind which guṇas can produce. These three states of mind are druti, deeptivistaar and vyaapakatva.

'Druti' in Sanskrit means 'to melt' or 'to flow'. When aesthetic pleasure leads to the melting of the heart, a person is said to be in a state of druti. A poem with maadhurya guṇa, for example, induces a state of druti in the reader. Druti, therefore, is a state of mind in which the hardness of the heart caused by such negative feelings as jealousy, hatred, and others, disappears. When shriNgaar, karuṇ and shaaNta rasas predominate in a poem the reader will experience druti.

Deeptivistaar is another state of mind. The word is a combination of 'deepti' ('light' or 'illumination') and 'vistaar', which means 'expansion'. Therefore, deeptivistaar indicates a state of mind which is characterised by a feeling of being liberated. Here, a person feels that their consciousness has suddenly expanded; they have come out of their limited self and become more intensely aware of the world around them. Rasas which lead to a state of deeptivistaar are veer (heroism and courage), raudra (anger) and vibhatsa (disgust). For example, when a person reads a poem that has veer rasa, they feel as if new energy were coursing through their veins. This is the state of deeptivistaar. Something similar happens in raudra and vibhatsa rasas also, although the nature of reaction is different in these rasas as anger and disgust are essentially different from heroism.

Vyaapakatva in Sanskrit means 'to bloom' or 'to grow'. Rasas which cause the vyaapakatva state of mind are those which bring about a sudden change in the emotional state of a person. These rasas are haasya (laughter), adbhut (wonder) and bhayaanak (fear). Laughter, wonder and fear affect us suddenly and we immediately react to them. We feel as if our emotions suddenly blossom. This state of vyaapakatva is sometimes combined with druti and sometimes with deeptivistaar.

The Three Guṇas: Maadhurya, Oja and Prasaad

Maadhurya

Maadhurya is the abstract noun derived from the adjective 'madhur' which means 'sweet'. This is a guṇa which produces a state of druti in the reader. It is created by the use of sweet-sounding words. To create this guṇa in their verse, the poet should avoid using long compound words and certain consonants such as the hard /t/. This guṇa produces a mellifluous quality in poetry. In the presence of this guṇa the reader is overcome with emotions such as love, sorrow and compassion. Mammat describes this guṇa as a certain kind of pleasure and writes:

> आह्लादकत्वं माधुर्यं शृङ्गारे द्रुतिकारणम्। (*काव्यप्रकाश*)
>
> aahlaadakatvaM maadhuryaM shriNgaare drutikaaraṇam |
>
> (*Kavyaprakash*)
>
> Maadhurya is that pleasure which is the cause of druti (melting of the heart) and is found in the shriNgaar rasa (the emotion of love).

Maadhurya guṇa is associated with three rasas: shriNgaar, karuṇ and shaaNta. ShriNgaar relates to love, especially those aspects that are concerned with meeting and parting. Karuṇ is concerned with the emotion of sorrow and shaaNta is a rasa associated with the absence of all desire. SaNyogashriNgaar rasa (the emotion of love when the lovers are together) contains the lowest level of maadhurya guṇa. ViyogashriNgaar rasa (when the lovers are separated) has more maadhurya than saNyogashriNgaar. Karuṇ rasa (sorrow) has a still higher level of maadhurya and shaaNta rasa has the highest level of maadhurya guṇa. Thus, when we move from a situation when the lovers are together to when they are separated, and then to a situation which causes sorrow and finally to a place when there is no desire left, we experience progressively increasing levels of druti, or melting of the heart.

Oja

The word oja means strength and energy. Vaman says in his *Kavyalankarsutra* that oja guṇa is the absence of laxity or dullness in a verse. The presence of oja guṇa in poetry makes the reader feel as if they were full of energy and their heart were burning. The reader also feels prompted to take action. To create oja guṇa in their verse, a poet should use long compound words and there should be an abundance of rough-sounding consonants such as the hard /t/, /th/, /d/ and /dh/. Mammat relates this guṇa to the veer rasa (bravery and heroism) and says:

> दीप्त्यात्मविस्तृतेर्हेतुरोजो वीररसस्थितिः। (*काव्यप्रकाश*)
>
> deepyaatmavistriteraheturojo veerarasasthitih | (*Kavyaprakash*)
>
> Oja causes the expansion of the burning heart and is found in veer rasa.

When a person feels that their heart has begun to burn and is being impelled to action, they are in a state of deeptivistaar. When this happens, it indicates the presence of oja guṇa. This guṇa is associated with veer, vibhatsa and raudra rasas. There is a progressively increasing level of oja in veer, vibhatsa and raudra rasa, in that order. In veer rasa there is a burning desire to defeat the adversary but in vibhatsa rasa there is a much stronger desire to run away from that which is disgusting. In raudra rasa, oja guṇa has the strongest intensity because in this situation there is a compelling desire to kill the enemy.

In the remaining three rasas—haasya (laughter), bhayaanak (fear) and adbhut (wonder) both maadhurya and oja guṇas can be present. If the haasya rasa is caused by love, there will be a predominance of maadhurya guṇa in it. If it is caused by the actions of a brave man (veer) there will be a predominance of oja in it. Similarly, in bhayaanak and adbhut rasas also the context decides whether maadhurya or oja will predominate.

Prasaad

According to Vaman, prasaad is that guṇa with the help of which a sentence's meaning in immediately made clear. This guṇa is nothing but the absence of verbosity or obscurity in language. Defining the features of prasaad guṇa, Mammat says:

> शुष्केन्धनाग्निवत् स्वच्छजलवत्सहसैव च,
> व्याप्नोत्यन्यत्प्रसादोऽसौ सर्वत्र विहितस्थितिः। (*काव्यप्रकाश*)
>
> shuShkendhanaagnivat swachhajalvatsahasaiva cha,
> vyaapnotyanyatprasaadoasau sarvartra vihitasthitih I (*Kavyaprakash*)
>
> As fire spreads through dry wood immediately and as water instantly makes wet the dry cloth, prasaad guṇa makes feelings like gentleness, peace and understanding suddenly spread through the heart. Prasaad guṇa is present everywhere, in all the nine rasas and in all literary works.

Prasaad guṇa is the quality of lucidity in poetry. When a poem makes its meaning clear to the reader without their having to make an effort, that poem is said to have prasaad.

Table 3.4: Relationship between guṇas and rasas

Guṇa	Nature of the guṇa	Associated rasas
maadhurya	sweetness; melting of the heart	shriNgaar, karuṇ, shaaNta
oja	energy and strength	veer, vibhatsa, raudra
prasaad	lucidity	all the nine rasas

CLASSIFICATION OF POETRY (BHEDAS)

Bhamah was the first scholar to provide a clear basis for classifying kaavya (a term used for all genres of literature such as poetry, drama and prose). In his *Kavyalankar* he says that we can classify kaavya according to four parameters: 1. Has the writer used meter?; 2. What is the language in which the work has been written?; 3. What kind of content does it have?; 4. What is the form in which it has been written?

1. Based on whether or not a piece of writing has meter, writing is classified as gadya (prose—that which does not have meter) and padya (verse—that which has meter).
2. When we classify literature on the basis of the language in which it has been written there are three types of kaavya: Sanskrit, Prakrit and Apabhramsh. In ancient times, Sanskrit was the standard language used in classical literature. Prakrit was also used for writing kaavya. Sometimes even in the same work (such as in the plays of Bhaasa and Kalidas) both Sanskrit and Prakrit were used. Prakrit was the common term used for a number of ancient (as well as medieval) vernacular dialects of northern and central India. It existed alongside Sanskrit. There was another class of non-Sanskrit languages which was called Apabhramsh. Since the time of Patanjali, Indian grammarians used the term Apabhramsh to denote the various dialects spoken in North India before the rise of modern north Indian languages. Literature was written in Apabhramsh as well. For example, the twelfth century Jain scholar, poet, grammarian, philosopher and logician Hemchandra wrote his texts in Apabhramsh. Thus, according to Bhamah, literature can be classified into Sanskrit, Prakrit (which includes Pali) and Apabhramsh.
3. Literature can also be classified on the basis of its content or subject matter. Bhamah says that a work based on a story taken from history constitutes one kind of kaavya called 'khyaatavritt'. If the story is completely imaginary, it is called 'kalpit'. If the subject of kaavya is based on some art

it is called 'kalaashrit' and if it is based on some shaastra or branch of learning, it is known as 'shaastraashrit'.

4. Literature can be classified on the basis of the form in which it has been written. Bhamah mentions a number of forms such as mahaakaavya, roopak or naatak, aakhyaayikaa, kathaa and so on. Mahaakaavya is an epic, while roopak (also called naatak) is a play. According to Bhamah, aakhyaayikaa is an interesting story which is written partly in prose and partly in verse. The language used in this form is simple so that it can be narrated orally. It is written on a noble subject and is divided into sections called uchchhwaas. By noble subject, Bhamah means a story of a man of noble character. In this kind of kaavya, the hero himself narrates his story and occasionally uses verse to describe events likely to happen in the future. Later, commenting on aakhyaayikaa, Dandin added that when the protagonist himself tells his story he is not allowed to describe his qualities and weaknesses. Events such as the kidnapping of a girl, a battle, separation of lovers and their final reunion are some of the common incidents described in an aakhyaayikaa. Kathaa, on the other hand, is written entirely in prose and is not divided into uchchhwaas. While an aakhyaayikaa can be written only in Sanskrit, a kathaa can be in Sanskrit, Prakrit or Apabhramsh. In a kathaa, the character of the hero is described by someone else.

Table 3.5: Bhamah's classification of kaavya

Basis of the classification	Types of kaavya
Use of meter	gadya (prose) and padya (verse)
Language in which the work is written	Sanskrit, Prakrit and Apabhramsh (dialect)
Subject on which it is written	khyaatavritt (a well known story), kalpit (an imaginary story), kalaashrit (a story about some art) and shaastraashrit (a story about some branch of learning).
Form	mahaakaavya (epic), roopak or naatak (drama), aakhyaayikaa and kathaa.

After Bhamah, Dandin divided kaavya into three categories—prose, poetry and that which is a blend of prose and verse called champoo. He says that of all these forms, drama is the finest. Vaman also categorises kaavya into prose and verse. He thinks that writing prose is a test of a poet's ability as it has no definite form. Vaman classifies kaavya into anibaddha kaavya and nibaddha kaavya. By anibaddha kaavya he means a work which is made up of a number of independent verses. Nibaddha kaavya, on the other hand, has a well-defined structure in which each part is related to what has gone before it and what comes after it.

Anandavardhan classifies kaavya on the basis of his theory of dhwani. Kaavya can be of three kinds: dhwani kaavya, guṇibhootavyangya kaavya and chitra kaavya. Dhwani kaavya, as its name suggests, is that in which dhwani, or the suggested meaning, is prominent. Such poetry is highly metaphorical and symbolic. Guṇibhootavyangya kaavya is that kind of poetry in which there is a suggested meaning, but it is secondary to the literal sense of the poem. In chitra kaavya there may be some figurative meaning, but it is completely overshadowed by the literal meaning of the poem.

Mammat accepts Anandavardhan's three-fold division of kaavya but names them differently. He calls them uttam, madhyam and avar kaavya respectively. For him, uttam kaavya is the best kind of poetry ('uttam' means 'the best'). In this kaavya the suggested meaning (dhwani) is more prominent than its literal meaning. For example, if we apply this principle to T.S. Eliot's *The Wasteland* we can say that it is uttam kaavya because it is predominantly symbolic. The second kind of poetry is madhyassma (average) kaavya. It may have a suggested meaning, but its literal sense is conveyed first. The third kind of poetry is avar kaavya (inferior poetry) in which there is hardly any metaphorical or symbolic meaning. Such poetry may have music, emotions and sweetness but Mammat considers it the lowest kind of poetry because it lacks nuances of meaning.

4

Words and Sentences

- Shabdashakti: the word's potential to convey meaning
- Taatparya vritti: structure and meaning of a sentence

SHABDASHAKTI: THE WORD'S POTENTIAL TO CONVEY MEANING

The shakti (power or potential) of a word (shabda) to convey meaning is known as shabdashakti. This power can be of three kinds. First, every word has the power to convey its literal meaning. If it cannot do this, it is not a word at all but a jumble of consonants and vowels. This power of a word to convey its literal meaning is called 'abhidhaa'. But a word can also suggest other kinds of meaning, that is, it has two other kinds of power to convey meaning. When a word indicates a meaning different from its literal meaning but related to it, it is known as its 'lakShaṇaa shabdashakti'. The third kind of shabdashakti is called 'vyaNjanaa'. When a word suggests a meaning that is different from either its literal or indicated meaning, it is known as its vyaNjanaa shabdashakti. We can also say that a word has three different modes of signification.

Many scholars of poetics such as Udbhat, Rudrat, Vaman and Rajshekhar have discussed shabdashakti in detail, but their focus has mainly been on abhidhaa and lakShaṇaa. With the emergence of the theory of dhwani in the ninth century, attention was paid to vyaNjanaa as well. Two major writers who deal with vyaNjanaa in great detail are Anandavardhan and Abhinavagupt.

Abhidhaa

As we have seen, when a word conveys its literal or primary meaning it is said to be in abhidhaa. The primary meaning of a word is called its mukhyaarth ('mukhya' means 'primary' and 'artha' is 'meaning'). While defining abhidhaa, Mammat says,

> स मुख्योऽर्थस्तत्र मुख्यो व्यापारोऽस्याभिधोच्यते। (*काव्यप्रकाश*)
>
> sa mukhyoarthastatra mukhyo vyaapaarosyaabhidhochyate ।
> (*Kavyaprakash*)
>
> The literal meaning of a word is its primary meaning and the word's function which relates to this primary meaning is called abhidhaa.

Thus, a word performing this function is said to have the abhidhaa shabdashakti. When a word is in abhidhaa it is known as a 'vaachak' and its meaning is called 'vaachyaarth', or 'literal sense'.

For example, when we say, 'There is a tiger in this forest', by 'tiger' we mean a certain kind of animal. In this sentence, 'tiger' is vaachak and its vaachyaarth is 'an animal of the big cat family which has black stripes on its body'. However, when we say, 'He was a tiger on the battlefield', we are not using the word 'tiger' in its literal sense. What we want to say is that on the battlefield he was as ferocious as a tiger. In this sentence, 'tiger' is not a vaachak because we are not using the word in its primary sense.

LakShaṇaa

LakShaṇaa is that function or power of a word, which enables it to convey an indicated meaning which, although related to its primary meaning, is different from it. Such a word is called 'lakShak' or a 'laakShaṇik' word and its meaning is known as its 'lakShyaarth'. While defining lakShaṇaa, Mammat says,

> मुख्यार्थबाधे तद्योगे रुढितोऽथ प्रयोजनात्,
> अन्योऽर्थो लक्ष्यते यत् सा लक्षणारोपिता क्रिया। (*काव्यप्रकाश*)
>
> mukhyaarthabaadhe tadyoge ruDhitotha prayojanaat,
> anyortho lakShyate yat saa lakShṇaaropitaa kriyaa । (*Kavyaprakash*)
>
> When the primary meaning of a word is rejected in favour of some other meaning, which is related to its primary meaning, the word is said to be in lakShaṇaa.

This new meaning is projected on to the literal meaning of the word. This new indicated meaning is conveyed by the word either because such meaning has been fixed by conventional use or because the speaker intentionally wants the word to convey that new indicated meaning.

When we want to describe someone as strong, ferocious or brave we often call them a tiger. In the sentence, 'He was a tiger on the battlefield', 'tiger' is in lakShaṇaa because it has not been used in its primary sense. It has been used in a sense that has been fixed by convention. Sometimes we ascribe a new meaning to a word because we want to. For example, in the lines 'Slowly, silently now the moon,/ Walks the night in her silver shoon', the poet describes the moon as a lady wearing silver shoes and crossing the sky. This meaning of the word 'moon' is not fixed by conventional use. The poet has intentionally used the word in this sense because he wishes to describe the beauty of the full moon by personifying it.

Let us take another example of lakShaṇaa. If someone says, 'The chair has ordered it', they are not referring to a piece of furniture but to the chairperson of the organisation where they probably work. Here the indicated meaning of the sentence is that the chairperson has ordered it.

LakShaṇaa is always dependent on abhidhaa, or the primary meaning of a word. Anandavardhan says that in lakShaṇaa we first understand a word in its primary sense, and after having rejected it, we understand it in its indicated sense. That is why scholars like Mammat have called lakShaṇaa the tail of abhidhaa. As the tail follows an animal, lakShaṇaa follows abhidhaa.

VyaNjanaa

VyaNjanaa, the third kind of shabdashakti, is completely different from lakShaṇaa. While lakShaṇaa is related to the primary meaning of a word (that is, to abhidhaa) vyaNjanaa is completely independent of it. That power of the word which helps it to express a meaning which is completely different from either its literal or indicated sense is called vyaNjanaa shabdashakti. We can also say that when we reject both the literal and indicated meanings of an expression and discover some hidden meaning in it, we have understood it as vyaNjanaa. The expression that conveys a hidden meaning is known as 'vyaNjak' and its meaning is called 'vyangyaarth'.

Before Anandavardhan, (the ninth century author of *Dhwanyalok* who propounded the theory of dhwani in Indian poetics) vyaNjanaa had not been regarded as a separate shabdashakti. It was he who declared for the first time that vyaNjanaa is a shabdashakti which is different from abhidhaa and lakShaṇaa. VyaNjanaa suggests the meaning of an expression while abhidhaa expresses its literal meaning and lakShaṇaa indicates a meaning that is different from its literal meaning, though related to it. Anandavardhan compares this suggested meaning to the beauty of a woman which is much more than the sum total of the loveliness of the different parts of her body. He also says that this suggested meaning is found in the works of great poets. He uses the term dhwani for this suggested meaning. We will learn more about dhwani in a later chapter.

Making a distinction between lakShaṇaa and vyanjanaa, Mammat says that the meaning of lakShaṇaa is understood because it has been fixed by conventional use, but when a poet uses vyaNjanaa he does it with the intention of conveying a hidden meaning to the cultivated reader.

VyaNjanaa has been classified into two broad categories: shaabdivyaNjanaa and aarthivyaNjanaa. ShaabdivyaNjanaa depends on the use of a particular set of words to convey the suggested meaning. If those words are changed, the vyaNgyaarth is lost. On the other hand, aarthivyaNjanaa does not depend on the words used in the expression. Even if they are replaced by their synonyms, the vyaNgyaarth is not lost.

The meaning of vyaNjanaa or its vyaNgyaarth depends on two factors: the context in which it has been used, and the sense in which the reader understands it. To take an example, if someone says, 'The sun has set', it could mean different things to different people. To a person whose practice it is to offer prayers every evening, it could mean that their time for prayer has come. To a night watchman it could suggest that he should now report for duty. When spoken to a woman at home, it could mean that she should begin cooking. To a student it could suggest that it is time to study.

And to the people living in a kingdom, it could mean that the king has died.

Let us take another example of vyaNjanaa. If someone says, 'Gangayam ghoshah' ('There is a hut in the Ganga'), it cannot be understood as abhidhaa as it is not possible to construct a hut in the middle of a river. This expression can only be understood either as lakShaṇaa or as vyaNjanaa. If understood in lakShaṇaa, the sentence means that there is a hut situated on the banks of the river Ganga. If understood as vyaNjanaa, the sentence could mean that the people living in that hut are extremely fortunate because they enjoy the cool breeze blowing across the river, or because they are close to such a holy river.

Table 4.1: Kinds of shabdashakti

Shabdashakti	Meaning	Example
abhidhaa	It is the primary meaning of a word.	'There is a tiger in the forest.'
lakShaṇaa	It gives a meaning different from the primary meaning of a word, where the new indicated meaning is related to the primary meaning.	'He was a tiger on the battlefield.'—meaning he fought ferociously in the battle
vyaNjanaa	It suggests a meaning different either from the primary or the indicated meaning of a word.	'Gangayam ghoshah.' (There is a hut in the Ganga.) suggesting the coolness and holiness of the dwelling

TAATPARYA VRITTI: STRUCTURE AND MEANING OF A SENTENCE

In Sanskrit, a sentence is made up of padas. When the grammatical marker of person, gender, number and case are added to a word, it becomes a pada. Such a marker indicating the grammatical function of a pada in a sentence is called 'vibhakti' in Sanskrit grammar. However, a random collection of padas will not constitute a sentence. If someone says, 'Cow horse sky tree', it is not a sentence as it does not convey any meaning. Therefore, our scholars of poetics asked themselves: What are the basic requirements of a sentence? They came up with three requirements which must be fulfilled *simultaneously* before a collection of padas can be called a sentence. We study these requirements under taatparya vritti. These requirements are yogyataa, aakaaNkShaa and sannidhi.

Yogyataa

Yogyataa requires that the padas used in a sentence must be related to one another in a logical manner. For yogyataa we must not use a pada that contradicts some other pada in the sentence. Rudrat states that padas in a sentence must be correlated to one another in an interdependent manner. Vishwanath uses the word yogyataa in the sense of the compatibility of padas with one another.

This can be understood with the help of an example. Let us take two sentences:

1. Water irrigates.
2. Fire irrigates.

'Water irrigates' is a perfectly meaningful sentence because the word 'water' does not contradict 'irrigates'. 'Fire irrigates' is meaningless because the word 'fire' contradicts 'irrigates'. The first sentence fulfills the requirement of yogyataa while the second collection of words fails to do so.

AakaaNkShaa

AakaaNkShaa literally means 'expectation'. The initial words in a sentence create an expectation of meaning in the listener which must be fulfilled. If a collection of words gives the impression that something is still left to be said, that is not a sentence because it does not fulfill the requirement of aakaaNkShaa.

When someone says, 'Water...' a number of questions may arise in the mind of the listener such as 'What about water?' or 'Water what?'. When the speaker adds 'is cool' the expectation or aakaaNkShaa of complete sense is fulfilled and the utterance has meaning. We can also say that when a number of words, spoken one after the other, are able to convey complete sense it is called a sentence.

Sannidhi

Sannidhi means the proximity of words in a sentence, spoken in such a way that there is no undue time lag between the pronunciation of one word and the word following it. For example, in the sentence 'Water irrigates' the two words must be spoken one after another in quick succession. For example, if a parent tells their child 'Your friend' and then adds after an hour, 'is coming today', they will not be understood because there is no sannidhi in what has been said. To fulfil the requirement of sannidhi they should have said, 'Your friend is coming today' pronouncing each word, one after the other in quick succession. Vishwanath has used the term aasakti for sannidhi.

Table 4.2: Requirements for a sentence

Requirement	Meaning
yogyataa	No word in a sentence should contradict some other word in it.
aakaaNkShaa	The listener's expectation of receiving complete meaning from the sentence must be fulfilled.
sannidhi	In a sentence, there should be no undue time lag between the utterance of one word and the next.

5

Rasa

- Features of rasa
- Bharat's theory of rasa
- Other theories of rasa
- Kinds of rasa

Rasa is one of the oldest concepts in Indian poetics. Bharat's *Natyashastra* is the first text which deals with the theory of rasa in comprehensive detail. 'Rasa' is a Sanskrit word with multiple meanings, some of which are 'juice', 'liquid' and 'taste'. Monomohan Ghosh, one of the translators of *Natyashastra*, uses the word 'sentiment' for 'rasa' while A.K. Coomaraswami prefers the term 'flavour' for it. The Rasa School is one of the six schools of Indian poetics, the other five being AlaNkaar, Reeti, Dhwani, Vakrokti and Auchitya.

Besides Bharat, other important scholars associated with the Rasa School are Bhattanayak, Lollat, Shrishankuk and Abhinavagupt. Even Bhamah and Udbhat, who belong to the AlaNkaar School, discuss rasa in some detail. Unlike Bharat though, they do not consider it the core element of poetry. Bhamah recognises rasa as an important element of poetry but considers alaNkaar to be its central feature which helps a reader to experience rasa. Udbhat expresses similar views on rasa.

Both Bhojdev and Mahim Bhatt, two major scholars of the Rasa School in the eleventh century, consider rasa to be the most important element of poetry. Besides discussing other aspects of poetics, Bhojdev's *Saraswatikanthabharan* and *Shringarprakash* deal with rasa in considerable detail and acknowledge it as the core element of poetry. Dhananjay's *Dasharupakam* also deals with rasa in drama. In the twelfth century we have a text called *Natyadarpana*, written jointly by Ramchandra and Gunachandra, asserting that rasa is the basic feature of poetry. We also have Sharadatanay's *Bhavprakashan* (thirteenth century) and Vishwanath's *Sahityadarpan* (fourteenth century) which are acknowledged as two major texts on rasa.

FEATURES OF RASA

Rasa, in Indian poetics, is essentially used to denote the emotional change which takes place in the sahridaya when they interact imaginatively with poetry or drama. The theory of rasa tries to explain this process.

Here we should keep in mind that it is not just anybody who can experience rasa. It can be experienced only by a sahridaya. Who is a sahridaya? The word has two parts: 'sa' ('with') and 'hridaya' ('heart'). So, 'sahridaya' literally means 'a person with a heart'. A person who is qualified to read and appreciate poetry is a sahridaya. They must be a cultivated reader. Our scholars have described a number of qualities a person should have in order to be called a sahridaya. They must be intelligent and sensitive. They must have acquired adequate knowledge of people and the world (loka) and must have been trained in and exposed to literature. Abhinavagupt says that a sahridaya is a person whose mind is like a mirror that has been cleansed by the constant study of poetry. They are also people who are capable of understanding what is being described in poetry. A sahridaya, thus, must have special qualities of mind and heart. It is the sahridaya who experiences rasa when they read poetry or watch a play. This happens because they are in a state of tanmayeekaraṇ with the text, meaning they have become one with it.

In order to experience rasa, the sahridaya must be a person in whom the sattva guṇa predominates. Indian philosophy identifies three states of consciousness called guṇas or qualities—tama (tamas), raja (rajas) and sattva in which tama is the lowest state of consciousness while sattva is the highest. A person in whom the tamoguṇa (literally 'darkness') predominates is characterised by ignorance, dullness, lethargy, inertia and inactivity. A person in whom the rajoguṇa is predominant is full of passion and activity.

A person in whom the sattva guṇa is prominent is known for their goodness of heart, purity of character and tranquillity of mind. Only such a person can experience rasa.

Experiencing rasa can make the reader a morally better person. Bhattanayak was the first to connect rasa with the spectator and discusses experiencing or taking in the flavour of rasa. He says that when a person experiences rasa they rise above tama and raja and attain sattva guṇa. Vishwanath says in his *Sahityadarpan*, 'Rasa, experienced by men of sensibility, is born of the dominance of the sattva principle, is indivisible, self-manifested, compounded of joy and consciousness, untouched by anything else perceived, akin to the realisation of God, and its very life is transcendental wonder'.

An important feature of rasa is that it is a unified and ceaseless experience. When we watch a play, we experience the emotions evoked by it. This is followed by a feeling of satisfaction resulting from what Vishwanath calls 'joy and consciousness'. Now, watching the play, feeling emotions and enjoying them take place almost simultaneously. Anandavardhan says that rasa is a unified emotional experience that connects the poet and the reader. It is an uninterrupted experience in the sense that while experiencing a literary text, the sahridaya does not experience vibhaavs (the determinants), anubhaavs (the consequents) and saNchaareebhaavs (fleeting emotions) separately or one after the other but enjoys them all together. When someone reads a poem, or watches a play, they do not know at which moment the awareness of art began, when it led to the stirring of emotions in them, and when it resulted in aesthetic pleasure. It all happens in a single flow of experience.

The end result of rasa is aanaNd or transcendental bliss. This aanaNd has been called alaukik by Abhinavagupt as it belongs to a plane of consciousness that is higher than the mundane. The word 'alaukik' literally means 'not of this world'. Again, the experience of rasa has also been called brahmaanaNd sahodar. 'BrahmaanaNd' means 'the bliss of experiencing the divine' and 'sahodar' means 'akin to'. Tasting rasa, therefore, is similar to experiencing the presence of God. And finally, as Bharat says, the rasa which poetry creates in the reader constitutes the ultimate meaning of poetry:

न हि रसादृते कश्चिदर्थः प्रवर्तते। (*नाट्यशास्त्र*)

na hi rasaadrite kashchidarthah pravartate I (*Natyashastra*)

Without rasa no meaning can ever be conveyed.

Table 5.1: Features of rasa

1.	Rasa is the emotional change in the reader brought about by poetry.
2.	Only a sahridaya or a cultivated reader can experience rasa.
3.	Rasa is experienced by a person in whom the sattva guṇa is predominant.
4.	Rasa is a unified and ceaseless emotional experience.
5.	The result of rasa is aanaNd or transcendental bliss.
6.	This aanaNd is akin to experiencing the divine (brahmaanaNd sahodar).
7.	Rasa constitutes the ultimate meaning of poetry.

BHARAT'S THEORY OF RASA

In his *Natyashastra*, Bharat explains how rasa is generated in the sahridaya. It is a process known as 'rasa niShpatti'. While discussing his theory of rasa he has used a number of terms which must be understood before we discuss the process. These terms are vibhaav, anubhaav, sthaayibhaav and saNchaareebhaav (also called vyabhichaareebhaav).

Vibhaav

The literal meaning of vibhaav is 'cause' or 'reason'. In a play, the cause of the stirring of emotion in the character, and consequently in the spectator is known as the vibhaav or determinant of the rasa. Vibhaavs can be called the causal factors of emotion. The person or thing which causes this emotion, is called the aalaMban vibhaav. The character who feels this emotion is called the aashray. Factors which intensify this emotion are called uddeepan vibhaavs ('uddeepan' means 'intensification').

For example, let us imagine that we are watching Kalidas's *Abhijnanashakuntalam*. In Act I, King Dushyant sees Shakuntala for the first time. Hidden behind a tree, he watches her. Shakuntala's friend Priyamvada praises her beauty. Shakuntala says it is flattery. On overhearing this conversation, King Dushyant says to himself:

> *King*: But the flattery is true.
> Her arms are tender shoots; her lips
> Are blossoms red and warm;
> Bewitching youth begins to flower
> In beauty on her form.
> (*Abhijnanashakuntalam* [trans. by Arthur W. Ryder], Act I, verse 17)

In this scene, Shakuntala is the aalaMban vibhaav because she is the cause of the stirring of the emotion of love in Dushyant, who is the aashray. The trees, vines, her 'bewitching youth' which 'begins to flower/In beauty on her form' intensify the feeling of love in Dushyant and therefore, they are uddeepan vibhaavs.

Anubhaav

'Anu' means 'that which follows'. In the presence of the aalaMban vibhaav the attendant actions of the aashraya, which reveal his or her feelings, are called anubhaavs. These are the consequents of the rasa. Bharat has used the word 'action' for anubhaav.

According to Bharat anubhaavs can be of two kinds. Some of the actions of the character are involuntary, while others are deliberate. The involuntary actions have been called saatvik bhaavs by Bharat. Through these saatvik bhaavs the feelings of the characters are expressed. The eight saatvik bhaavs mentioned by Bharat have been described in the table below.

Table 5.2: Saatvik bhaavs

Saatvik bhaavs	Meaning of the word	Emotions causing it
stambha	inability to move	excessive joy, fear, sorrow or embarrassment
swed	perspiration	fear or shyness
romaaNch	getting goose bumps	joy, fear or shyness
swarabhaNg	breaking of the voice	excessive sorrow, fear or joy
vepathu	trembling	anger, excessive joy or fear

(*Contd.*)

Table 5.2: (*Contd.*)

Saatvik bhaavs	Meaning of the word	Emotions causing it
vaivarNya	the face becoming pale	sorrow, fear, anxiety
ashru	shedding tears	joy and sorrow
pralaya	fainting	sorrow, fear, separation from one's beloved

The characters can also express their feelings with the help of deliberate actions which include expressions, gestures, body language, speech and costume. These anubhaavs are called kaayik or bodily actions.

To go back to the example given above, the kaayik (bodily) anubhaavs include those actions of Dushyant which express his feelings for Shakuntala. His soliloquy is an example of this kind of anubhaav. When he praises the beauty of her arms and lips in such glowing terms, the spectator understands that he is in love.

Anubhaavs are essential for the generation of rasa. The mere presence of characters on the stage does not generate rasa. They have to act convincingly in order to convey their emotions to the spectators. Only then will the spectator also feel the emotions and rasa generated in them. But in order to taste the rasa of the play, the spectator has to go through the process of tanmayeekaraṇ. It means that they have to forget themselves and identify completely with what is happening on the stage.

Sthaayibhaav and SaNchaareebhaav

Both sthaayibhaav and saNchaareebhaav refer to emotions. Bharat has identified eight sthaayibhaavs or primary emotions. We may also call these emotions dominant emotions which characterise each rasa. These eight sthaayibhaavs are love, mirth, sorrow, anger, enthusiasm, fear, disgust and wonder which correspond to shriNgaar, haasya, karuṇ, raudra, veer, bhayaanak, vibhatsa and adbhut rasas respectively. From the beginning of the play till its end, these sthaayibhaavs remain in the spectator till they are converted into rasa. We shall have more to say about these different rasas later.

Bharat has described other kinds of emotions which are transitory in nature. These are saNchaareebhaavs, also known as vyabhichaareebhaavs. In any given situation, there is one dominating emotion (sthaayibhaav) and a number of transitory emotions (saNchaareebhaavs) which come and go but are in fact related to the same domination emotion.

For example, let us imagine that a character in a play suddenly sees a big cobra facing him. Feeling very frightened, the man stops in his tracks. In this situation, fear is the sthaayibhaav or the dominating emotion. As he stands facing the cobra, he begins to feel anxious about his well-being and therefore experiences a sense of anxiety. But then after a while he begins to hope that perhaps the cobra will go away and he will be saved. So, after the feeling of anxiety comes the feeling of hope. But again, he looks at that big cobra and begins to feel a sense of panic because the thought of being killed by the snake returns. So, after feeling hopeful for a while, he begins to feel a sense of terror. Thus, a number of emotions rise in him. There is anxiety about his well-being, a momentary hope of getting away safely and then the panic caused by the thought of dying. All these emotions are saNchaareebhaavs because they are transient. But all the while the dominant emotion, fear, remains the same. In this situation, fear is the sthaayibhaav and anxiety, hope and terror are saNchareebhaavs. When this primary emotion of fear (bhay) becomes manifest as rasa, we call it bhayaanak rasa.

We can take another example. Let us assume that a play shows a man in love. Here the sthaayibhaav is love but the emotion of love gives rise to other feelings which come and go. The lover may feel a sense of despair because his beloved is away, or he may feel elated when he sees her again, or he may have doubts about the possibility of winning her hand, and so on. Although the lover feels all these saNchaareebhaavs, the dominant emotion or sthaayibhaav remains the same, which is love, and the rasa the situation evokes in the spectator is shriNgaar rasa.

Apart from the eight sthaayibhaavs or primary emotions, Bharat has also mentioned thirty-three saNchaareebhaavs. These transitory emotions are the following: discouragement, weakness, apprehension, envy, intoxication, weariness, indolence, depression, anxiety, distraction, recollection, contentment, shame, inconstancy, joy, agitation, stupor, arrogance, despair, impatience, sleep, epilepsy, dreaming, awakening, indignation, dissimulation, cruelty, assurance, sickness, insanity, death, fright and deliberation. It is surprising that 'death' appears on this list. We usually perceive death as a condition of the body and not a feeling. However, here 'death' means the feelings a person has when he watches someone's death, learns about it or thinks about it. Depending on the situation, these saNchareebhaavs can be associated with any of the eight sthaayibhaavs.

The Generation of Rasa

The generation of rasa, or rasa niShpatti, is a complex process. It is not correct to say that rasa is generated when the poet 'communicates' emotions to the reader. Emotions cannot be 'communicated' to the reader if the poet simply names them. In fact, the emotions a spectator feels during a dramatic performance *belongs* to them; the playwright has not 'communicated' them to the spectator. What the playwright has done is that by the force of their writing and by creating suitable objective correlatives they have awakened emotions already present in the spectator.

Bharat says that rasa niShpatti takes place when vibhaavs, anubhaavs and vyabhichaareebhaavs (also called saNchaareebhaavs) come together.

> विभावानुभाव व्यभिचारिसंयोगाद् रस-निष्पत्तिः। (*नाट्यशास्त्र*)
>
> vibhaavaanubhaav vyabhichaarisaNyogaad rasa-niShpattih ।
> (*Natyashastra*)
>
> The combination of vibhaav, anubhaav and vyabhichaaribhaavs generates rasa.

When these three are present simultaneously, the sthaayibhaav in the spectator is awakened and rasa is experienced. For the success of a play or a poem, the formation of rasa is absolutely essential because if it does not happen, the play or the poem has failed to convey its essential meaning. (see p. 69 for Bharat's quote)

Bharat compares the process of experiencing rasa to the pleasure of tasting food. He says that the taste of food is the result of a combination of different spices and ingredients. Just as there are six kinds of taste (sweet, sour, salty, bitter, pungent and astringent), there are different kinds of rasas. Rasa niShpatti means the experience of 'feeling' the sthaayibhaav by the reader or spectator. It is similar to tasting and enjoying food. The primary emotion, such as love or sorrow, is already familiar to the spectator of a play as a result of their experiences in this world. When they watch the actors representing emotions on the stage with the help of their words, expressions and gestures, the spectator also feels that emotion. Bharat writes,

> यथा बहुद्रव्ययुतैर्व्यंजनानि बहुभिर्युतम्,
> आस्वादयन्ति भुंजानाः भुंक्ते भुक्ताविदोजना।
> भावाभिनय संयुक्ता स्थायिभावास्ततो बुधाः,
> आस्वादयन्ति मनसा तस्मान्नाट्ये रसाः स्मृताः। (*नाट्यशास्त्र*)
>
> yathaa bahudravyayutairvyaNjanaani bahubhiryutam,
> aaswaadayanti bhuNjaanah bhuNkte bhuktaavidojanaa ।
> bhaavaabhinay saNyuktaa sthaayibhaavaastato budhaah,
> aaswaadayanti manasaa tasmaannaaTye rasaah smritaah ।
> (*Natyashastra*)
>
> As people who appreciate the taste of food enjoy eating food cooked with various condiments, in the same manner sahridayas enjoy the rasa of drama when they taste the sthaayibhaav born out of vibhaav, anubhaav and saNchaareebhaav.

The only difference between savouring food and experiencing rasa is that while the former involves the tongue, rasa is a complex mental activity. Abhinavagupt says,

> न रसनाव्यापार आस्वादनम् अपितु मनसा एवम् स चात्रविलोकस्ति।
> (*अभिनवभारती*)
>
> na rasnaavyaapaar aaswaadanam, apitu manasa evam, sa chaatravilokasti । (*Abhinavabharati*)
>
> Taste is concerned with the tongue, but the experience of rasa is related to the mind.

Later scholars discussed rasa niShpatti in the light of the theory put forward by Bharat. Mammat, for example, explains the process of the generation of rasa in the following manner:

> कारणान्यथ कार्याणि सहकारीणि यानि च,
> रत्यादेः स्थायिनो लोके तानि चेन्नाट्यकाव्योः।
> विभावानुभावास्तत् कथ्यन्ते व्यभिचारिणः,
> व्यक्तः स तैर्विभावाद्यैः स्थायी भावो रसः स्मृतः। (*काव्यप्रकाश*)
>
> kaaraṇaanyatha kaaryaaṇi sahakareeṇi yaani cha,
> ratyaadeh sthaayino loke tani chennaatyakaavyayoh ।
> vibhaavaanubhaavaastat kathyante vyabhichaariṇah,
> vyaktah sa tairvibhaavaadyaih sthaayee bhaavo rasah smritah ।
> (*Kavyaprakash*)
>
> In this world, the causes (woman, pleasant surroundings, and others) of the awakening of emotions such as love which live permanently in the hearts of the people, and their effect in terms of actions, and their attendant feelings are called vibhaav, anubhaav and vyabhichaareebhaav respectively if these are described in a play or a poem. Rasa is said to be the emotion aroused in the heart of the sahridaya by the suggestive power of all these.

Vishwanath in his *Sahityadarpan* also describes the process of rasa niShpatti. He believes that the moment rasa niShpatti takes place, tamoguṇa and rajoguṇa in the sahridaya are destroyed and sattva guṇa becomes prominent. While answering the question of whether rasas such as karuṇ can be the cause of distress in the spectator, Vishwanath says that no rasa can cause distress. It always leads to transcendental bliss. If people would really become unhappy watching sorrow being enacted on the stage, no one would watch a play like the Ramayana.

OTHER THEORIES OF RASA

Bhattalollat's Utpattivaad

Bhattalollat, who lived in the tenth century, wrote an extremely perceptive commentary on Bharat's *Natyashastra*. He considers the question: Where does rasa originate? In other words, he is asking:

does rasa originate in the characters depicted in the play, or in the actors playing those characters, or in the spectator of the play? His answer to this question is known as the theory of utpattivaad (or the theory of the origin of rasa). According to him, the beginning (utpatti) of rasa is in original characters such as Rama, Dushyant, Shakuntala and others described in poetry. When actors dressed in the right kind of costume enact the characters, the feelings of the characters are projected on to the actors. What the actors do and how they express feelings on stage are merely projections of the actions and feelings of the original characters. Therefore, rasa originates in the characters described in drama and there is no rasa in the heart of the spectator. There is only the pleasure given by rasa that resides in the spectator.

Shrishankuk's Anumitivaad

Criticising the theory of utpattivaad, Shrishankuk put forward another theory about the origin of rasa. This is known as the theory of anumitivaad, a word that comes from 'anumaan' meaning 'conjecture', 'assumption' or 'imagining one thing to be another'. Shrishankuk says that when we see an actor playing a character like Rama, Dushyant or Shakuntala, we imagine the actor to be the character he or she is playing. For some the duration of the drama or poem we take our imagination to be reality. Vibhaavs, anubhaavs and saNchaareebhaavs are the factors which help us imagine that the actor is the original character and rasa is the result of this imagination.

The theory of anumitivaad invites comparison with what S.T. Coleridge, the English Romantic poet and critic, has to say about 'poetic faith'. He believes that when reading or writing poetry it is important that we practise 'that willing suspension of disbelief for the moment, which constitutes poetic faith'. Coleridge believes that while reading a poem the reader should temporarily accept the author's vision as true in order to enjoy their poetry. Shrishankuk also believes that, by making use of their imagination, the spectator of a play accepts the actors on stage as the characters they are portraying. When the spectator does this, they are able to experience rasa.

Abhinavagupt's Abhivyaktivaad (or the Theory of Expression)

While discussing rasa, Abhinavagupt goes beyond the theories of both utpatti (origin) and anumiti (conjecture or assumption) and puts forward another theory which came to be known as abhivyaktivaad. He says emotions such as love, laughter, sorrow, anger, enthusiasm and others exist as sthaayibhaavs in every person. A person's experience of living in this world gives them familiarity with these emotions. Under normal circumstances these emotions are dormant in a person. When there is a combination of vibhaavs, anubhaavs and saNchaareebhaavs, these sthaayibhaavs are expressed or become manifest (abhivyakt). The pleasure of experiencing these emotions is called rasa. Rasa, therefore, is not something that originates anywhere else (as Bhattalollat claims), nor is it the result of the assumption that the actor is the character he is playing (as Shrishankuk believes), it is something that is always present, but dormant, in a person and only manifests under certain circumstances, such as when they are watching a play.

Explaining the meaning of sthaayibhaav, Abhinavagupt says that in the heart of the spectator some vaasanaas are present as saNskaar. Very broadly, saNskaar means the basic personality traits of a person. Vaasanaa is the influence of a person's good and bad deeds on their consciousness. These influences are generally unconscious. We could say that vaasanaas are those subconscious tendencies in a person which are the result of their own actions, and which in turn determine the nature of their future actions. Hindu philosophy believes that fundamentally it is a person's vaasanaas that decide whether they will be happy or unhappy in his life. These vaasanaas create a person's saNskaar or basic character, which may be morally good or bad. The implication of this theory is that a person can never escape the consequences of their actions (karma), whether good or bad. The consequences of their actions result in their growth or degeneration as a moral being.

Now when a good actor plays a character on the stage, they succeed in expressing the feelings of the character they are portraying.

For example, an actor playing the role of Rama is able to project the emotions of the hero of the Ramayana. As a result of this projection, the spectator experiences similar emotions that are lying dormant in them because of the combined power of vibhaav, anubhaav and saNchaareebhaav. But what is the nature of this emotion experienced by the spectator? Abhinavagupt says that as a result of watching a play when a spectator experiences sorrow for example, that experience of sorrow has nothing to do with the memory of some personal sorrow they have experienced in the past. The drama-generated sorrow is not limited by the spectator's own personal experience of sorrow. The spectator experiences this kind of art-generated emotion by a process of generalisation (saadhaaraṇeekaraṇ) which helps them rise above their limited self. The saNskaar which enables the spectator to feel the emotions of the character being presented on the stage is already present in the spectator, but when they watch the actors on the stage the saNskaar becomes manifest as rasa. The example of an earthen pitcher has often been given by various scholars to explain this phenomenon. The smell of the earth is already present in a dry earthen pitcher but when it comes into contact with water, that smell manifests and we notice it. Thus, Abhinavagupt considers rasa to be something that is expressed or manifests due to a literary event involving the text, whether it is read or performed, and the sahridaya.

For Abhinavagupt rasa is central to literature, and alaNkaar, auchitya, guṇas and other such literary devices and qualities merely support the generation of rasa. His conclusion, therefore, is that rasa resides in the heart of the sahridaya and nowhere else. He also says that because the emotions felt during a dramatic performance are not bound by space and time and are the same for all spectators of the play, they are extremely intense and transcendental, transporting the spectators into some other world. As a result of his exposure to literature, the sahridaya rises above their limited self and petty sense of personal joys and sorrows and shares a universalised emotion with all around them. This experience is sublime and divine.

Barriers to experiencing rasa according to Abhinavagupt

Abhinavagupt believes that everyone does not experience rasa every time they watch a play or read a poem. There are situations in which the literary text fails to generate any rasa in a person. He mentions seven barriers to experiencing rasa. In the following situations a person will not experience any rasa, and consequently, will get no pleasure from art. We will consider these situations in the context of drama.

1. *SaMbhaavanaavirah*: If the play describes something which is impossible to believe, the spectator will not experience any rasa. In other words, the play should be able to convince the spectator that what is being shown on the stage can actually happen.
2. *Swa-pargat-desh-kaal-visheShavesh*: While watching a play if a spectator is reminded of their own personal experiences of place and time, they will fail to experience any rasa and will get no pleasure from the play. To enjoy the play the spectator has to forget themselves.
3. *Nijasukhadivivashibhaav*: This condition is an extension of the previous one. If the spectator is in a disturbed emotional state while watching a play it will act as a barrier to their enjoyment of rasa. In other words, if they are concerned with their own emotions, they will not experience aesthetic pleasure.
4. *Pratyutpaayavaikalya*: If the means by which rasa is generated are faulty or incomplete the spectator will not experience rasa.
5. *Sphutwaabhaav*: If the elements generating rasa are not expressed clearly no rasa will be generated.
6. *Apradhaanata*: If the play highlights its secondary and not primary elements, it will act as a barrier to the experiencing of rasa.
7. *SaNshayayoga*: If the writer fails to establish a clear relationship between vibhaavs, anubhaavs and saNchaareebhaavs

on the one hand and the sthaayibhaav on the other, the spectator will not experience any rasa. The play must be written well for rasa to be generated.

Saadhaaraṇeekaraṇ or the Generalisation of Emotion

Bhattanayak is the first scholar to have used the term saadhaaraṇeekaraṇ to describe what happens during the process of the generation of rasa. He believes that rasa is generated in the spectator by this process of saadhaaraṇeekaraṇ, or the generalisation of emotion. The word 'saadhaaraṇ' means 'common' or 'general' and 'saadhaaraṇeekaraṇ' means 'making something common or general'. Thus, the meaning of saadhaaraṇeekaraṇ is that the particularity or uniqueness of vibhaavs and anubhaavs is lost and they become common. When a person watches a play, the characters appearing on stage look unique in the beginning, but as they continue to watch it, this uniqueness is gradually lost. At the same time, the spectator loses consciousness of their own limited self and is able to identify with the characters. It is then that the spectator experiences rasa. To understand this, we need to go back to the passage from Kalidas's *Abhijnanashakuntalam* we quoted earlier. When the play begins and Dushyant and Shakuntala appear on the stage, they are specific people with whom the spectator is familiar because they have read the Mahabharat. They see Dushyant as the king of Hastinapur and ancestor of the Kuru clan, and Shakuntala as the girl brought up by Rishi Kanva and the woman who later became the mother of the great Emperor Bharat. But after a while, both Dushyant and Shakuntala, who are being represented on the stage by the actors, lose their individuality. They become a young man and a young woman who are in love with each other. This happens because of the process of saadhaaraṇeekaraṇ. Bhattanayak says that drama has that power by which the feelings and emotions of a character in a play become the feelings and emotions of the spectator. Abhinavagupt and Dhananjay too embrace the theory of saadhaaraṇeekaraṇ and refine it further.

KINDS OF RASAS

Rasas can be of different kinds depending on the dominant emotions to which they are related. Bharat discusses eight rasas: shriNgaar (love), haasya (mirth), karuṇ (sorrow), raudra (anger), veer (bravery), bhayaanak (fear), vibhatsa (disgust) and adbhut (wonder). Later, some more rasas were added to this list. Of these eight, Bharat identifies four as the primary rasas. These primary rasas are shriNgaar, raudra, veer and vibhatsa. The other four rasas are related to these primary rasas. Bharat says that haasya is related to shriNgaar, karuṇ to raudra, adbhut to veer and bhayaanak to vibhatsa. Explaining the relationship between these rasas, he says that imitating erotic love (shriNgaar) on stage results in laughter (haasya). Fury (raudra) ends in sorrow (karuṇ). The heroic (veer) causes a sense of wonder (adbhut) and the odious (vibhatsa) leads to fear (bhayaanak).

ShriNgaar

Bharat rates shriNgaar rasa very highly and says, 'Whatever is sacred, pure, tranquil and worth-seeing can be compared to shringaar' (*Natyashastra*). Rudrat also considers this rasa very important and writes in his *Kavyalankar* that it is the most pleasing of all the rasas and has the capacity to touch everyone, from a child to an old man. Without it, he continues, poetry is neeras or unattractive. Anandavardhan says that of all the rasas, shriNgaar rasa is the sweetest and the most exhilarating.

'Rati' or 'erotic love' is the sthaayibhaav (dominant emotion) of shriNgaar rasa. It concerns men and women in the fullness of their youth. According to Bharat, the vibhaavs (determinants) which result in and intensify this rasa include meeting one's beloved in a garden or in a splendid mansion and playing and dallying with him or her. This feeling is also heightened when the characters are wearing bright and beautiful clothes. Elements that intensify this rasa are pleasant seasons and the characters wearing garlands, ornaments and makeup.

ShriNgaar rasa is of two kinds: saNyogashriNgaar (union of lovers) and viyogashriNgaar (their separation). These two kinds of shriNgaar are also called saMbhogashriNgaar and vipralambhashriNgaar respectively. The anubhaavs (consequents) of saNyogashriNgaar include the movement of the eyes and eyebrows, casting loving glances at each other, moving limbs in a soft and delicate manner and speaking to each other in a sweet voice. SaNchaareebhaavs (transitory emotions) such as fear, indolence, cruelty and disgust are completely excluded from saNyogashriNgaar. ViyogashriNgaar refers to the feelings of the lovers when they have been separated. Its anubhaavs (consequents) are showing indifference, languor, jealousy, fatigue, anxiety, yearning, drowsiness, sleep, dreaming, illness, insanity, epilepsy and death.

According to Bharat, shriNgaar can be represented on stage in three ways: through speech, by wearing the right kind of clothes and by suitable actions. By this he probably means that the sentiment of love may be conveyed to the spectators if the characters speak in a sweet voice, wear bright and beautiful clothes and their expressions, gestures and body language suggest that they are in love.

Haasya

Haasya rasa is related to laughter which is also its sthaayibhaav. Bharat says that this rasa is caused by determinants (vibhaavs) such as wearing funny-looking clothes behaving in an impudent manner, displaying greediness, quarrelling with another character in a slapstick manner, talking nonsense and similar acts which make us laugh. He adds that a character can represent this emotion on the stage by moving their lips rapidly, twitching the muscles of their nose and cheek, opening their eyes wide or contracting them, showing that they are perspiring, suddenly changing the look on their face, and holding their sides while laughing. These are the anubhaavs (consequents) of this rasa. Haasya can be of two kinds: first, when the character himself or herself is laughing, and second, when he or she is the cause of laughter in other people.

Bharat describes six kinds of laughter, obviously to be used by an actor to play different kinds of characters. He mentions smit (a slight smile), haasit (smile), vihaasit (gentle laughter), upahaasit (laughter of ridicule), apahaasit (vulgar laughter), and atihaasit (excessive laughter). In smit, the teeth should not be visible while smiling. In haasit, the teeth can be seen but only slightly. Vihaasit should have a low, sweet sound and should be suitable to the occasion. In upahaasit, the nostrils are expanded, the eyes are squinting and the shoulders and head are bent forward. Laughter not suitable for the occasion, that which brings tears to the eyes or that which makes the shoulders and head shake violently, is called apahaasita. Atihaasit is that kind of laughter in which the eyes are wide open, the person is making a very loud sound and is holding their sides. Bharat says that the first two kinds of laughter (smit and haasit) indicate a superior kind of person. The next two kinds (vihaasit and upahaasit) are associated with an average person and the last two kinds (apahaasit and atihaasit) indicate a person of inferior character.

Karuṇ

Karuṇ rasa evokes sadness and therefore its sthaayibhaav (dominant emotion) is sorrow. Bharat says that the vibhaavs which contribute to the generation of this rasa include suffering because of a curse, being away from one's dear ones, seeing someone die, losing one's wealth, being in captivity, being forced to leave one's home, meeting with an accident, and similar sorrowful happenings. The character on stage can express this sentiment with the help of such anubhaavs as shedding tears, wailing, feeling dry in the mouth, face turning pale, feeling weak in the limbs, feeling out of breath, and so on. The saNchaareebhaavs associated with this rasa include languor, anxiety, delusion, fainting, fear, tremor, loss of voice, and so on. Karuṇ rasa can be classified into three categories: the sadness a person feels when they are prevented from doing what is lawful, the sorrow caused by the loss of a person's wealth, and finally, the feeling of sadness at someone's death.

Raudra

Raudra rasa is related to anger and therefore krodh is its sthaayibhaav. According to Bharat, raakShasaas (demons), daanavaas (demons) and arrogant men display this emotion. The vibhaavs of this rasa include being insulted, facing false allegations, being raped, being threatened, feeling an urge to take revenge, fighting with someone, feeling jealous and other situations which make a person angry. The anubhaavs of this rasa include beating up people, breaking and crushing things, picking up weapons, wounding someone with a weapon, fighting, drawing blood, and similar violent acts. On stage, an actor can express this emotion by displaying red eyes, knitting their brows, biting their lips, shaking the muscles of their cheeks, pressing one hand hard against the other, and so on. The saNchaareebhaavs of this rasa are determination, energy, restlessness, indignation, fury, perspiration and trembling of the limbs. In reply to the question of 'Do only raakShasaas and daanavaas get angry?', Bharat says that other people can also get angry, but anger is the characteristic trait of a raakShasaa.

Veer

Veer rasa is related to heroism and courage and its sthaayibhaav is utsaah or enthusiasm. Bharat says that this rasa is always associated with a person of noble character. The vibhaavas of this rasa include the character showing presence of mind, displaying perseverance, behaving in a diplomatic manner, showing discipline, displaying military strength, expressing aggressiveness, having the reputation of being a mighty person, and so on. The character onstage can represent this sentiment by such anubhaavs as showing firmness, patience, heroism, charity and similar other qualities associated with a person of superior virtue. The saNchaareebhaavs associated with this rasa include self-assurance, pride, judgment, energy, ferocity and indignation.

Veer rasa is generated under three conditions: first, when we see a daanaveer or a person doing charity; second, when we see a dharmaveer or a person doing his duty; and third, when we see a yuddhaveer or a person fighting his enemy. It is obvious from this that veer rasa is the sentiment that arises in us when we see a person of noble character in action. The nobility of character is expressed by their generosity (doing charity), honesty (doing his duty) and courage (fighting his enemy). The main difference between raudra rasa and veer rasa is that when a person is angry they lose their sense of discretion, while the brave person always retains this ability.

Bhayaanak

Fear is the sthaayibhaav of bhayaanak rasa. Bharat says that the vibhaavs which create this rasa include hearing loud noises, seeing ghosts, seeing some ferocious animal, finding oneself in a vacant house, being alone in a forest, seeing someone's death, watching someone in captivity, or even hearing about someone's death or captivity. He adds that an actor can represent this emotion on stage by the trembling of their hands and legs, face turning pale, losing their voice and similar actions suggesting panic. These are the anubhaavs of this rasa. The saNchaareebhaavs associated with bhayaanak rasa include feeling paralysed, perspiring, being unable to speak, feeling restless and anxious and becoming inactive. Bharat says that these are the changes noticed in the behaviour of a person when he is frightened. Bhayaanak rasa can be represented on stage in three ways: with speech, appropriate costumes and action. Bharat also identifies three situations that can evoke bhayaanak rasa. First, a person may only pretend to be frightened. Secondly, they may be actually afraid because they have done something wrong; and thirdly, they may be afraid of some impending danger.

Vibhatsa

Disgust is the sthaayibhaav of vibhatsa rasa. According to Bharat, seeing impure or disgusting things, hearing about them, or even talking about them are the vibhaavs of this rasa. Vibhatsa rasa can be represented on stage by such anubhaavs as the immobility and numbness of the limbs, drawing the lips together, vomiting, spitting, expressing disgust by a gesture of the hands, and similar actions suggesting revulsion. The saNchaareebhaavs associated with this rasa include epilepsy, delusion, agitation, fainting, feeling sick, or death. Vibhatsa rasa can be of three kinds: normal, nauseating and exciting. A person normally feels a sense of aversion when they are exposed to something odious. Then there is the nauseating feeling caused by the sight of worms or excrement. And finally, when a person sees blood or other things related to war they feel excitement of a certain kind, which is also related to vibhatsa rasa.

Adbhut

Astonishment is the sthaayibhaav of adbhut rasa. This rasa is associated with the feeling of awe and wonder. Vibhaavs that can generate this rasa include seeing heavenly beings or events, getting a desired object, entering a grand building, temple or an audience hall (sabhaa), seeing acts of magic or those events which can create an illusion. Its anubhaavs include opening the eyes wide, gazing at something continuously and rapturously, getting goose bumps, shedding tears of joy, perspiring, speaking words of praise, moving fingers to show wonder, and similar actions. The saNchaareebhaavs associated with this rasa are feeling uneasy, experiencing a breaking of the voice, getting agitated, acting in a hurried manner, and so on. Bharat says that adbhut rasa can be of different kinds. If a person says something wonderful, it may cause this rasa. Again, we may feel a sense of wonder when we meet a person of exceptionally noble character. Adbhut rasa is also created when we witness something remarkably surprising. And finally, we feel a sense of wonder when we see a person who is exceptionally good looking.

According to Bharat adbhut rasa can be further classified as celestial and joyous. Here the word 'celestial' means seeing heavenly things on stage. For example, if gods and goddesses appear as characters in a play it will generate adbhut rasa of the celestial kind. When something happy takes place in a person's life and they feel that life is wonderful, this feeling is the adbhut rasa of the joyous kind.

Colours and deities associated with various rasas

Bharat associates these eight rasas with different colours. He is probably suggesting that the predominance of a specific colour on stage may help in the creation of a particular mood or emotion. According to him, light green is best suited for shriNgaar; white is the colour of haasya rasa; karuṇ rasa goes with grey; raudra is related to red; veer is associated with light orange or saffron; bhayaanak goes with black; vibhatsa is related to blue; and adbhut is highlighted by yellow.

Bharat has also mentioned that fact that each rasa has a presiding deity from the Hindu pantheon. Vishnu, the protector, is the presiding deity of shriNgaar rasa. Pramathaas (the gaṇas or ghosts and sundry other spirits of Shiva) are the presiding deities of haasya rasa. The presiding deity of karuṇ rasa is Yama who is the god of death. Rudra (Shiva in a destructive mood) is the presiding deity of raudra rasa. The word 'raudra' comes from Rudra. The god of veer rasa is Indra. He is one of the most important Vedic gods and represents courage, energy, heroism and optimism. The deity associated with bhayaanak rasa is Yama, the god of Death. Mahaakaal is the presiding deity of vibhatsa rasa. Mahaakaal is another name for Shiva and represents not only his victory over time and death, but also the truth of the presence of death in this world. Mahaakaal has also been seen as the destroyer of darkness and evil. And finally, Brahma is the presiding deity of adbhut rasa. This is probably because it is Brahma who has created this wide and wonderful world, which is a perennial source of awe and wonder.

Table 5.3: Kinds of rasas

Rasa	Sthaayibhav (dominant emotion)	Associated Colours	Associated Deities
shriNgaar	rati (love and eroticism)	light green	Vishnu
haasya	haas (laughter)	white	the Pramathaas
karuṇ	shok (sorrow)	grey	Yama
raudra	krodh (anger)	red	Rudra
veer	utsaah (enthusiasm)	saffron	Indra
bhayaanak	bhay (fear)	black	Yama
vibhatsa	jugupsa (disgust)	blue	Mahaakaal
adbhut	vismaya (astonishment)	yellow	Brahma

Later additions to the list of eight rasas

Over the course of time, other rasas were added to the original list of eight proposed by Bharat. In the ninth century, Rudrat mentions preyan rasa for the first time and after him Bhojdev also discusses it in some detail. In his *Kavyalankar*, Rudrat says that the essential element of preyan is sneh (love, which is non-conjugal). He says that when there is sneh between two people there is love, faith, the wish for each other's well-being and sweet conversation. He adds, 'Their eyes moisten because of the tenderness of the heart and they look towards each other with eyes full of joy'. Thus, by sneh Rudrat means an affectionate and innocent relationship between two friends. However, Bhojdev explains sneh differently. For him, sneh is the sentiment that characterises the relationship between the hero and the heroine of a play. There seems to be a question about whether the nature of preyan rasa is sexual or non-sexual. Many later scholars do not consider preyan to be a rasa.

The existence of another rasa called shaaNta rasa was proposed by later scholars. Bhattataut, a tenth century scholar and Abhinvagupt's guru, considers shaaNta rasa to be the greatest of all rasas because it is akin to gaining salvation or mokSh. Anandavardhan thinks that shaaNta is the primary rasa in the Mahabharat. Its sthaayibhaav is 'shama' or 'nirved' which means 'the absence of all desire'. Ramchandra and Gunachandra in their *Natyadarpana* say that shama represents the equilibrium of the mind, freedom from desire, greed, fury, ego, illusion and attachment to worldly affairs.

The existence of another rasa called vatsal rasa was also suggested. Its sthaayibhaav is vaatsalya. Vaatsalya is the affection that a parent has for their child, or that which a teacher has for their student. It also means the affection shown by elders to younger members of the family. The meaning of the term extends even to the affection that adults have for children, even if the children are not related to them. Bhojdev and Vishwanath have accepted the existence of this rasa. Its aalaMban vibhaavs are the son, daughter, pupil or a child. According to Vishwanath the intensifying factors (uddeepan vibhaav) of this rasa include the child's lisping, the son or daughter's good education, his or her courage or compassion for others, the success of the student, and similar things that make a parent or teacher proud. The anubhaavs of this rasa include touching the head of the child, picking it up, embracing it, watching the son, daughter or student with pride, and so on. The saNchaareebhaavs of this rasa are pride, joy, attraction, worry for the child's well-being and associated emotions.

In his *Bhaktirasamritasindhu*, Roopgoswami writes about ujjwalbhakti rasa, or the bright sentiment of devotion. The sthaayibhaav of bhakti rasa is love and devotion to a deity. The aalaMban vibhaav of this rasa is god or any object of worship. Its intensifying factors include thinking about god, praising god, meeting other devotees and so on. Its anubhaavs include singing the praise of god, shedding tears, dancing and weeping.

There is some controversy about whether bhakti rasa should be considered a rasa or not. Abhinavagupt does not think that there can be any other rasa except the nine rasas (including shaaNta rasa) traditionally mentioned. He goes to the extent of saying that the feeling of devotion does not constitute a separate rasa and it is wrong to consider it so. Some scholars say that bhakti rasa is covered by shaaNta rasa. Panditraj Jagannath however thinks that bhakti and shaaNta rasas are not the same as they represent opposite states of the mind: devotion is the opposite of being without desire. In conclusion we can say that from Bharat to Panditraj Jagannath, most scholars have recognised only nine rasas.

6

AlaNkaar

- Meaning of alaNkaar
- Kinds of alaNkaars

MEANING OF ALANKAAR

An alaNkaar is a figure of speech. It is a word or phrase that is used in a non-literal sense to make writing more vivid. The Sanskrit word 'alaNkaar' means 'ornament' or 'embellishment', and therefore when we use the term in the context of literary writing, we are suggesting that the writer has 'embellished' their language with the help of certain literary devices.

We can understand the difference alaNkaars make to writing with the help of an example. Let us take these lines from William Wordsworth's well-known poem on daffodils. We remember how he describes himself as wandering 'lonely as a cloud / That floats on high o'er vales and hills' when he sees daffodils growing thick on the bank of a lake. He writes,

> Continuous as the stars that shine
> And twinkle on the milky-way,
> They stretched in never-ending line
> Along the margin of a bay:
> Ten thousand saw I at a glance,
> Tossing their heads in sprightly dance.
>
> (William Wordsworth, *Daffodils*)

Here the poet compares the daffodils to the stars in the Milky Way. Flowers and stars have nothing in common and normally it would be absurd to compare them. But the poet wishes to suggest more than what an ordinary statement like 'The daffodils were countless and bright' would have meant. Therefore, he uses an upamaa (simile) and by saying that the daffodils remind him of the stars in the Milky Way he is suggesting that they are as numerous and as bright as the stars. Since he has used the image of the sky in the day in the previous stanza, he wants to evoke again the image of the sky, though this time at night. He achieves this special effect by using an upamaa. Because an alaNkaar can change the very character of a statement, our scholars have always considered it a very important aspect of poetic expression.

After Bharat (who also discussed alaNkaars, though not at such length as later scholars), this area of study developed as a separate discipline and continued to flourish till it reached its zenith in the sixth and seventh century CE when Bhamah and Dandin, two of the most influential scholars of the AlaNkaar School, wrote their seminal texts on the subject. Bhamah's *Kavyalankar* and Dandin's *Kavyadarsh* deal with all the usual topics in poetics, but their primary focus is on alaNkaars. These texts show that by the seventh century, alaNkaar had established itself as the main subject of discussion in Indian poetics. Efforts were also made to classify alaNkaars. While Bharat had mentioned only four alaNkaars, their number grew to over a hundred with the passage of time.

In the sixth century, Bhamah defined alaNkaar thus:

वक्राभिधेया शब्दोक्तिरिष्टा वाचामलंकृतिः। (काव्यलंकार)

vakraabhidheyaa shabdoktiriShTaa vaachaamalaNkritih ।
(*Kavyalankar*)

The oblique expression of the word-meaning combine is called alaNkaar.

He says that alaNkaar is an expression that is vakra or oblique. It means that it is not the kind of language people normally use in their daily life. By making their expression vakra, the poet makes it striking and beautiful. When a poet uses alaNkaars in poetry they are able to create a sense of chamatkaar or wonder, in the reader. AlaNkaar, therefore, is the main reason why poetry looks beautiful. He says that as ornaments enhance the beauty of a woman, alaNkaars add to the beauty of poetry.

In the next century, Dandin also linked the use of alaNkaars to poetic beauty and wrote:

> काव्यशोभाकरान् धर्मान् अलंकारान् प्रचक्षते। (*काव्यदर्श*)
>
> kaavyashobhaakaraan dharmaan alaNkaaraan prachakShate ।
>
> (*Kavyadarsh*)
>
> Elements that add loveliness to poetry are known as alaNkaar.

Vaman, who lived in eighth century CE, seems to disagree with the view that alaNkaars are the primary cause of poetic beauty. He says:

> काव्यशोभायाः कर्त्तारो धर्मस्तु गुणाः,
> तदतिशयहेतवस्त्वलंकाराः, सौन्दर्यमलंकारः। (*काव्यालंकारसूत्रवृत्ति*)
>
> kaavyashobhaayaah karttaaro dharmastu guṇaah,
> tadatishaayahetavstavalaNkaaraah, saundaryamalaNkaarah ।
>
> (*Kavyalankarsutravritti*)
>
> Elements that add beauty to poetry are the guṇas, and for intensifying that beauty there are alaNkaars. Beauty itself is alaNkaar.

It is obvious from this that for Vaman poetic beauty is the result of the various kaavyaguṇas (the qualities of poetry). In Chapter 3 we saw how guṇas like maadhurya (sweetness), oja (energy) and prasaad (lucidity and overall charm) give a distinct flavour to poetry. Vaman seems to suggest that when we mention the factors which make poetry beautiful and striking, we must mention guṇas before alaNkaars.

After Vaman, scholars also discussed the relationship between alaNkaar and rasa. The general view is that alaNkaars may help in the creation of rasa but as Mammat says, rasa can be evoked even without them. In his *Kavyaprakash* he says that alaNkaars may contribute to the creation of rasa, but then he qualifies his statement by adding that they are not always necessary for rasa. He uses an analogy in which he says as ornaments add to the loveliness of a beautiful woman, alaNkaars add to the intensity of rasa. If a woman is not beautiful though, ornaments cannot make her lovely. Similarly, if a poem has no innate capability of evoking rasa, no amount of embellishment with alaNkaars can generate rasa. AlaNkaars can only provide a superficial glow to the poem, but they cannot add anything to its emotional content. Further, he says that sometimes it may happen that there is rasa in a poem but despite the use of alaNkaars the rasa is not intensified. This happens because the poet has not used the right kind of alaNkaars for that rasa. As inappropriate ornaments do not add to the beauty of even a lovely woman, the wrong use of alaNkaars do not add to the rasa of a poem.

There is no unanimity among scholars about the exact number of alaNkaars. Bharat mentions only four of them while Bhamah and Dandin discuss over thirty. Vaman names and explains thirty-three kinds of alaNkaars while Udbhat raises their number to forty-one. Udbhat also classifies them into six categories. Rudrat, a ninth century scholar, names and explains fifty-two different kinds of alaNkaars and by the time we come to Mammat in the eleventh century, their number goes up to sixty-seven. The number of alaNkaars increased and in the fourteenth century Vishwanath describes seventy-seven alaNkaars while Jaydev names a hundred. In Appaya Dikshit's *Kuvalayanand* we come across the names of a hundred and twenty-four alaNkaars. It suggests that careful work was done in this field and major alaNkaars were subdivided into more and more categories.

From the beginning, alaNkaars were considered a very important element in literary writing. Bharat discusses them in the context of drama and believes that no dramatic performance is possible without using alaNkaars. He believes that alaNkaars are the basis of drama:

> उपमा रूपकं चैव दीपकं यमकं तथा,
> अलंकारास्तु विज्ञेयाः चत्वारोनाटकाश्रयः। (*नाट्यशास्त्र*)
>
> upmaa roopakaM chaiva deepakaM yamakaM tathaa,
> alaNkaaraastu vigyeyaah chatvaaro naaTakaashrayah | (*Natyashastra*)
>
> Upmaa, roopak, deepak and yamak are the four kinds of alaNkaars which are the basis of drama.

Similarly, Kuntak, the founder of the Vakrokti School, considers alaNkaar to be one of the central elements of poetry. Vagbhatt also says that despite having guṇas and being free from defects, poetry cannot create chamatkaar or a sense of wonder if no alaNkaars have been used in it. Jaydev says that as there is heat in fire, there should be alaNkaar in poetry. Mammat considers alaNkaars to be important, although he concedes that poetry may succeed even without them, provided there are guṇas in it. Mahim Bhatt, on the other hand, believes that both guṇas and alaNkaars add to the beauty in poetry.

TYPES OF ALANKAARS

Scholars have classified alaNkaars into different types. Bharat mentions four alaNkaars but does not classify them. It was in the sixth century that Bhamah became the first scholar to classify them and created two categories into which they can be placed. He called these categories 'shabdaalaNkaar' (alaNkaars related to words) and 'arthaalaNkaar' (alaNkaars related to meaning). Over the course of time, another category called 'ubhayaalaNkaar' was created. 'Ubhaya' means 'both' and 'ubhayaalaNkaar' means a figure of speech which is a combination of two or more different kinds of alaNkaars. In this combination, there can be two shabdaalaNkaars, or two arthaalaNkaars, or one shabdaalaNkaar and another arthaalaNkaar. Since ubhayaalaNkaar combines both the primary kinds of alaNkaars, a discussion of shabdaalaNkaars and arthaalaNkaars will naturally cover it.

ShabdaalaNkaar

'Shabda' in Sanskrit means 'word' and alaNkaar is a figure of speech and therefore, shabdaalaNkaar means a kind of alaNkaar which depends on the use of a particular word or a set of words. If we replace that word with its synonym, the alaNkaar will be lost and the expression will not have the meaning it earlier had. Some of the most common shabdaalaNkaars have been discussed below.

Anupraas

When a particular consonant is repeated twice or more in the same word, it is known as anupraas. The vowel sounds may be different, but the consonants have to be the same.

The repetition of a particular consonant helps in the creation of a particular rasa and therefore there is a relationship between the repetition of a specific consonant and the creation of an emotional state in the reader.

Anupraas has been subdivided into various types depending on the nature of the consonant being repeated, how many times it has been repeated, whether these consonants come at the beginning of the words or at their end, or even on the basis of whether words or sentences are being repeated. Anupraas can be of two main types:

1. *Varṇaanupraas*: When a particular varṇa (consonant) is repeated in a line, it is an example of varṇaanupraas. If a consonant is repeated only once, it is called chekaanupraas but when it is repeated many times, it is called vrityaanupraas.
2. *Shabdaanupraas*: When a particular shabda (word) is repeated in a line, it is an example of shabdaanupraas. In such an alaNkaar the same word is used in different senses in the line.

Some scholars like Udbhat call it padaanupraas also. 'Pada', as we have seen before, means a word to which the required grammatical marker has been added to show its function in a sentence. Shabdaanupraas can also be of two kinds. When only one pada is repeated it is known as ekpadgatshabdaanupraas, but when a number of padas are repeated it is known as anekpadgatshabdaanupraas.

Even the repetition of an entire line in a poem can be called anupraas, but the repeated lines should have different meanings. This kind of anupraas is known as laataanupraas.

Although the English term 'alliteration' does not cover the various kinds of anupraas we have in Sanskrit, we can use this term to describe anupraas generally.

The following lines can be taken as an example of varṇaanupraas:

> The **f**air breeze blew, the white **f**oam **fl**ew,
> The **f**urrow **f**ollowed **f**ree.
>
> ('The Rime of the Ancient Mariner', S.T. Coleridge; emphasis added)

Here, the anupraas or the repetition of the /f/ sound helps to recreate the sound made by the wind and the waves.

The following lines are an example of shabdaanupraas:

> यस्य च सविधे दयिता दवदहनस्तुहिनदीधितिस्तस्य,
> यस्य न सविधे दयिता दवदहनस्तुहिनदीधितिस्तस्य।
>
> (*सुभाषितानि, नायिका महिमा*)
>
> yasya cha savidhe dayitaa davdahanstuhinadeedhitistasya,
> yasya na savidhe dayitaa davdahanstuhinadeedhitistasya.
>
> (*Subhashitani*, Nayika Mahima)
>
> For the man whose beloved is away from him, the cool moon is like the forest fire. For the man whose beloved is with him, even the forest fire is like the cool moon.

Here the entire line has been repeated. The only difference between the two lines is that while in the first line 'cha' has been used in the second line there is 'na' in its place.

Yamak

Yamak is an alaNkaar in which a word or phrase is repeated in a sentence, but the word or phrase means something different each time it appears. The term in Western poetics which corresponds to yamak is antanaclasis. Dandin says that the repetition of a consonant–vowel combine is known as yamak. Defining yamak, Mammat says that when a word is repeated a number of times and has a different meaning each time it is called yamak.

For an example of yamak in English drama we can refer to Othello's speech in *Othello*, Act V, Scene 2. Othello enters Desdemona's bedroom with the intention of killing her because he is convinced that she has been unfaithful to him. A small candle burns in the room. He says to himself:

> It is the cause, it is the cause, my soul.
> Let me not name it to you, you chaste stars,
> It is the cause. Yet I'll not shed her blood,
> Nor scar that whiter skin of hers than snow
> And smooth as monumental alabaster.

Yet she must die, else she'll betray more men.
Put out the **light**, and then put out the **light**.
(*Othello*, Shakespeare; emphasis added)

In the example above, we see that in the last line the word 'light' has been repeated but the word has a different meaning each time it appears. The first 'light' has been used in its literal sense and refers to the candle burning in Desdemona's room. The first 'put out the light' means 'put out the candle' so that there is darkness in the room and Othello cannot see Desdemona's face. But the second time Othello uses the word 'light' he does it in a figurative sense. The second 'put out the light' means 'kill Desdemona'.

ShleSh

The word 'shleSh' comes from a root which means 'to stick'. When a word is used in such a way that it has two meanings at the same time it is called shleShaalaNkaar. This is called paronomasia or pun in Western poetics.

To take an example from English poetry:

Wilt thou forgive that sin where I begun,
Which was my sin, though it were done before?
Wilt thou forgive that sin, through which I run,
And do run still, though still I do deplore?
When thou hast done, thou hast not **done**,
For I have more.
('A Hymn to God the Father', John Donne; emphasis added)

Here in the fifth line the word 'done' has two meanings at the same time. The first 'done' is the past participle form of the verb 'to do'. The second 'done' has the same sound as 'Donne', which is the name of the poet. Therefore, the line 'When thou hast done, thou hast not done' has two meanings: (a) When you have forgiven my sins there will still remain some sins to be forgiven (something will remain to be 'done'); and (b) When you have forgiven all my sins, even then John Donne, being extremely sinful, will not be fit to be received by you.

There is a difference of opinion about whether shleSh is primarily a shabdaalaNkaar or an arthaalaNkaar. Bhamah considers shleSh to be an arthaalaNkaar. Udbhat also describes shleSh as an arthaalaNkaar but he classifies it into two groups: arthashleSh and shabdashleSh. Mammat has taken shleSh to be both arthaalaNkaar and shabdaalaNkaar. Ruyyak, on the other hand, has taken shleSh to be an arthaalaNkaar.

ShleShaalaNkaar can be of two kinds: 'shabdashleSh' and 'arthashleSh'. ShabdashleSh is a figure of speech which relates to the use of particular words, while arthashleSh is related to meaning. In shabdashleSh, poetic brilliance is created by the use of a word with two meanings, and if that word is replaced by its synonym the brilliance is lost. In the example given above, if the word 'done' is replaced by 'forgiven' the shleShaalaNkaar will be lost because only 'done' rhymes with 'Donne'.

Contrary to this, in arthashleSh although the word used has only one meaning, it conveys two or more senses naturally. Even if we replace that word with its synonym, the shleShaalaNkaar is not lost. Let us see an example of arthashleSh:

Turning and turning in the widening gyre
The falcon cannot hear **the falconer**;
Things fall apart; the centre cannot hold;
Mere anarchy is loosed upon the world,
The blood-dimmed tide is loosed, and everywhere
The ceremony of innocence is drowned;
The best lack all conviction, while the worst
Are full of passionate intensity.

('The Second Coming', W.B. Yeats; emphasis added)

The second line mentions 'falcon' (a bird used in hunting) and the falconer (the man who controls it and whom it obeys). But the context of the poem suggests that these words are an arthashleShalaNkaar and have some other meaning. When the extended sense of these words is considered, the 'falcon' probably represents all of humanity, while the 'falconer' means some kind of controlling authority which can maintain order in the world. The line then means that people ('the falcon') have stopped obeying any kind of authority ('the falconer') which can preserve moral order in the world. The consequence of this breakdown of order is that 'things fall apart' and there is moral anarchy in the world. We come to this meaning only when we explain the use of 'falcon' and 'falconer' as an arthashleShalaNkaar.

Vakrokti

When a person makes a statement meaning it in one sense but the listener understands it in another sense, such a statement is called vakrokti alaNkaar.

Vakrokti can be of two types: shleSh and kaaku. In shleSh vakrokti a word with multiple meanings is used and the listener takes a meaning which is different from the intended meaning of the speaker. In kaaku vakrokti, the listener takes a meaning different from the intended meaning of the speaker because of the tone in which the statement is made. For example, let us imagine that someone is waiting for a specific person. After a long wait, when the person finally arrives, the first person says to them, 'You are very punctual'. Obviously, the second person will not take this statement to be praise but will understand that the first person is irritated by their being late. Such a statement is an example of vakrokti, or irony.

Punarukti

When the same word or a group of words is repeated, it is known as punarukti (or 'saying it again'). By repeating a word or a phrase the poet wants to achieve a particular effect. The following lines by Lord Tennyson can be taken as an example:

> **Half a league, half a league**,
> **Half a league** onward,
> All in the **valley of Death**
> **Rode the six hundred**.
> "Forward, the Light Brigade!

Charge for the guns!" he said.
Into the **valley of Death**
Rode the six hundred.

('The Charge of the Light Brigade', Lord Tennyson; emphasis added)

The repetition of 'half a league' suggests that every soldier is riding forward continuously. It also conveys a sense of speed by recreating the rhythm of the galloping horses' hooves. Punarukti, therefore, adds a new dimension to the meaning of lines in poetry.

ChitraalaNkaar

'Chitra' means picture and there are times when a poet arranges the verse in such a manner on the page that they form some kind of shape or picture. For example, the poet might write a poem in which each line of the verse has a different number of words and when the poem is written it forms the shape of a tree, or a temple. This is known as chitraalaNkaar. This alaNkaar is counted among the shabdaalaNkaars because it relates to the written form of the word and not to its meaning. This alaNkaar does not enhance any rasa, but it certainly shows the skill of the poet.

Table 6.1: Common shabdaalaNkaars

ShabdaalaNkaar	Meaning
anupraas	repetition of a consonant sound in a line in order to create a particular effect
yamak	repetition of a particular word in such a manner that each time it means something different
shleSh	using a word in such a manner that it conveys two different meanings at the same time
vakrokti	when a person makes a statement in one sense and the listener understands or takes it in another sense
punarukti	repeating the same word, or a group of words, in a line in poetry.
chitraalaNkaar	arranging words typographically on a page in such a manner that some shape is created

ArthaalaNkaar

ArthaalaNkaar is another broad division of alaNkaars. As its name suggests, this kind of alaNkaar does not depend on the use of specific words but on the artha, or meaning, of the entire statement. In arthaalaNkaar it is sometimes possible to replace a word with its synonym and the function of the alaNkaar will not change, provided the meaning of the expression does not change.

Like shabdaalaNkaars, arthaalaNkaars too are of various types. Most of these types involve making comparisons, showing difference, highlighting paradoxes or underscoring contradictions and irony. The following are some of the most common arthaalaNkaars.

Upamaa

Upamaa, or simile, is one of the most widely used alaNkaars in poetry. In this kind of alaNkaar there is an explicit comparison between two distinctly different things which are not related as cause and effect. It should have the following four elements:

1. The comparison must be made between two things that are different in kind.
2. Despite the difference, the two things must have some sort of similarity between them.
3. Upamaa must clearly highlight this similarity.
4. This similarity is expressed with the help of words such as 'like', 'as', 'as if', and other such words and phrases.

The two things that upamaa brings together for comparison are known as 'upamaan' and 'upameya'. Upamaan is that which is being compared to something else while upameya is the thing or person to which the upamaan is being compared. The poet finds a common quality in the upamaan and upameya and this common quality is highlighted with the help of words such as 'as', 'like', and other similar terms.

The following lines from Valmiki's Ramayana (the *Sundarkaand*) have upamaa alaNkaar in them:

दुष्करं निष्प्रतिद्वन्द्वं चिकीर्षन् कर्म वानरः,
समुदग्रशिरोग्रीवो गवां पतिरिवाबभौ।

> duShkaraM niShpratidwandwaM chikeerShan karma vaanarah,
> samudagrashirogreevo gavaaM patirivaababhau ।
>
> Hanuman wanted to do that which is difficult for others and in this task there was no one to help him. He lifted his head and neck. At that moment, he looked like a well-built, muscular bull.

Here, Hanuman is the upamaan and 'well-built, muscular bull' is the upameya. Similarly, Matthew Arnold in these lines from 'Dover Beach' uses upamaa alaNkaar:

> Ah, love, let us be true
> To one another! for **the world**, which seems
> To lie before us **like a land of dreams**,
> So various, so beautiful, so new,
> Hath really neither joy, nor love, nor light,
> Nor certitude, nor peace, nor help for pain;
> And we are here as on a darkling plain
> Swept with confused alarms of struggle and flight,
> Where ignorant armies clash by night.
>
> (emphasis added)

Here, 'the world' (which is the upamaan) is compared to 'a land of dreams' (which is the upameya) and 'like' is the word which suggests a similarity between 'the world' and 'a land of dreams'. Upamaa, therefore, shows some similarity between two things. This similarity may pertain to quality (guṇa) or to shape (aakriti)—that is, it can be guṇakritisamaashraya.

Bharat has mentioned four kinds of upamaas:

1. comparing one thing to one thing,
2. comparing many things to one thing,
3. comparing one thing to many things,
4. comparing many things to many things.

Further, he has identified five situations in which an upamaa can be used: first, while praising someone or something; secondly, to criticise someone or something; thirdly, to describe something imaginary; fourthly, to indicate similarity; and finally, using an upamaa involving things that are only slightly similar.

Upamaa has also been classified into a large number of subtypes depending on variations in its different components.

Roopak

For Bharat roopak is an alaNkaar in which the thing being compared (upameya) and the thing to which it is compared (upamaan) are seen as one and the same. Roopak is an implied comparison and unlike upamaa, the comparison is not explicitly stated. Therefore, words such as 'like' or 'as' are not used. The English term for roopak is metaphor. Roopak has been classified into a number of subtypes on the basis of the function of or the emphasis on its different components.

In the following verse from the *Rigveda*, roopak alaNkaar has been used:

ये चिद्धि मृत्युबन्धव आदित्यामनवः स्मसि,
प्र सू न आयुर जीवसे तिरेतन।

ye chiddhi mrityubandhava aadityaamanavah smasi,
pra soo na aayur jeevase tiretana ।

O Adityas, as we men have death for our companion and friend,
May you lengthen our days on earth, so that we may live.

In this verse, roopak alaNkaar has been used because death is seen as man's companion and friend (baNdhu). This roopak suggests that people in Vedic times faced the reality of death in an unperturbed and undaunted state of mind. This roopak does not express the escapist belief that death is an illusion or only sleep, which other roopaks used for death do. Here, death has been called man's companion because it is always with man. Thus, a roopak can convey an idea in a succinct manner.

To take another example of roopak from William Shakespeare:

There is a **tide** in the affairs of men,
Which, **taken at the flood**, leads on to fortune:
Omitted, all the voyage of their life
Is bound in **shallows** and in miseries.

(*Julius Caesar*, Act IV, Scene 3, William Shakespeare; emphasis added)

Here 'tide' is a roopak for favourable opportunities in life. 'Taken at the flood' is a roopak for doing something at the right time. If a person does something at the right time, they will be successful, but if they 'omit' the tide, their ship will be in the 'shallows'. Here 'shallows' is a roopak for failure and misery.

UtprekShaa

Imagining one thing as another and expressing it by using 'as if' or 'as though' is utprekShaalaNkaar. Let us take an example:

> लिम्पतीव तमोऽङ्गानि वर्षतीवाञ्जनं नभः,
> असत्पुरुषसेवेव दृष्टिर्विफलतां गतः । (*काव्यादर्श*)
>
> limpateeva tamoaNgaani varShateevaaNjanam nabhah,
> asatpuruShaseveva driShtirvifalataaM gatah । (*Kavyadarsh*)
>
> It seems as if darkness had coated my limbs; as if the sky were raining black unguent and my eyes are of no use to me, as serving an evil man is of no use to a person.

To take another example: 'Her **eyes** looked **as if they were lotuses.**' Here the poet imagines that her eyes are lotuses, although the poet also suggests that they know they are different. They only remind them of the flower. Thus, to imagine the upameya in the upamaan is utprekShaalaNkaar. In this alankar expressions such as 'as if' or 'as though' are used.

UtprekShaalaNkaar can be of various types. Two of the most common types of this alaNkaar are vastutprekShaa and hetutprekShaa. When one thing is imagined to be present in another (as in the example given above) it is vastutprekShaa. For instance, in one of his couplets, the great Hindi poet Bihari compares the dark-skinned Krishna to a mountain of neelmaṇi (blue sapphire) and his yellow clothes to the light of the morning sun. Here he is using utprekShaalaNkaar because he uses the word 'manau' (as if) in the couplet to indicate that, although he is comparing Krishna to a mountain of blue sapphire and his yellow clothes to the morning sun, he knows that they are not the same. Yet when he imagines Krishna, he is reminded of a mountain of blue sapphire which is glowing in the morning sun.

When a poet uses the hetutprekShaalaNkaar they make it seem as if a certain situation is the cause of an event—a situation which may not actually be true. We can understand this with the help of an example. In his poem *Padmavat*, Malik Muhammad Jayasi says that the sun which shines with a thousand rays set in shame when he saw the glowing forehead of the beautiful Padmavati. This is an example of hetutprekShaalaNkaar because the setting of the sun has not actually been caused by the beauty of Queen Padmavati. With the help of this alaNkaar, Jayasi is suggesting that when the sun sets, it becomes red. The poet imagines that this redness of the sun has been caused by shame. The sun is full of shame because even its light is not as bright as the forehead of Padmavati.

Atishayokti

Atishayokti alanNkaar, or hyperbole, is a deliberate exaggeration while describing something. Let us take these lines from *Hamlet* where the hero says:

> I loved Ophelia;
> **Forty thousand brothers**
> Could not, with all their quantity of love,
> Make up my sum.
> (*Hamlet,* Act V, Scene 1, William Shakespeare; emphasis added)

The expression 'forty thousand brothers' is an atishayokti alaNkaar.

To take another example of this alaNkaar:

> **One impulse from a vernal wood**
> May teach you more of man,
> Of moral, evil and of good,
> Than all the sages can.
> ('The Tables Turned', William Wordsworth; emphasis added)

Here the poet exaggerates the power of nature to teach. He says that one little gust of wind from a forest in springtime can teach us more about moral behaviour, evil and good than all the sages and their books. This too is an example of atishayokti alaNkaar.

Vyaajstuti

This is an alaNkaar in which the surface meaning of the words used is the opposite of what is actually intended. For instance, the speaker may appear to be praising someone while they are actually being critical, or *vice versa*. Vyaajstuti is a kind of irony.

To take an example:

> I fear I wrong the **honourable men**
> Whose daggers have stabb'd Caesar, I do fear it.
>
> (*Julius Ceasar*, Act III, Scene 2, William Shakespeare; emphasis added)

There is vyaajstuti in 'honourable men' because men who stabbed a defenceless man (Julius Caesar) cannot be honourable. The real meaning is that such men have no sense of honour.

Virodhaabhaas

Virodhaabhaas is a statement which appears to be contradictory and yet turns out to have a valid meaning. Virodhaabhaas is what is known as paradox in English.

For example, virodhaabhaas alaNkaar has been used in the following lines:

> One short sleep past, we wake eternally,
> And death shall be no more; **death thou shalt die.**
>
> ('Death, Be Not Proud', John Donne; emphasis added)

The virodhaabhaas here is in 'death thou shalt die'. On the face of it, this statement seems absurd because death is a condition in which something living ceases to have life. Therefore, it is meaningless to say that death itself will die. But despite this contradiction, the sentence has a perfectly valid meaning. The poet says that when he considers the fact that death is like a short sleep after which there is eternal life, it ceases to frighten him, and it is in this sense that death will die.

Table 6.2: Common arthaalaNkaars

ArthaalaNkaar	Meaning
upamaa	an explicit comparison between two distinctly different things (simile)
roopak	an implied comparison between two things (metaphor)
utprekShaa	imagining one thing as another (a special kind of metaphor)
atishayokti	a deliberate exaggeration while describing something (hyperbole)
vyaajstuti	where the surface meaning of the words used is the opposite of what is actually intended (a kind of irony)
virodhaabhaas	a statement that appears to be contradictory and yet turns out to have a valid meaning (paradox)

7

Reeti

- Vaman and the theory of reeti
- Meaning of reeti
- Types of reeti

VAMAN AND THE THEORY OF REETI

Almost a century before Vaman, Dandin had described the features of reeti in his *Kavyadarsh*, but it was Vaman who raised it to the level of a major critical approach. Vaman asserts that reeti is the soul of poetry, which is to say that other elements of poetry such as rasa, alaNkaar, guṇa, et cetera can be explained only in terms of reeti. In the first five chapters of his *Kavyalankarsutra*, he offers arguments to prove the centrality of reeti in poetry. He writes:

> रीरिरात्मा काव्यस्य। (*काव्यालंकारसूत्र*)
>
> reetiraatmaa kaavyasya | (*Kavyalankarsutra*)
>
> Reeti is the soul of poetry.

Here it is interesting to consider the etymology of the words aatmaa (soul) and reeti. Aatmaa has been derived from the root 'aat' which means 'to move'. It has also been suggested that the word might have come from the root 'aan' which means 'to live'. Aatmaa, therefore, has connotations of both 'movement' and 'life'. Reeti has been derived from the root 'ri' which also means 'to move'. Therefore, when Vaman calls reeti the aatmaa of poetry, he is saying that reeti is the moving principle of poetry without which it is lifeless.

Poetic Beauty, AlaNkaars, Guṇas and Reeti

It will help us understand the concept of reeti if we consider the correlation between poetic beauty, alaNkaars, guṇas and reeti.

Achieving poetic beauty is the primary aim of every poet. Vaman states in unambiguous terms that the defining feature of kaavya is beauty. Now what is the cause of this beauty? Vaman says that the guṇas of poetry cause its beauty and those elements which enhance that beauty are alaNkaars.

We have already seen that there are three guṇas of poetry: maadhurya, oja and prasaad. AlaNkaars are the poetic devices which enhance the beauty of a poetic composition. When the relative roles of guṇas and alaNkaars in creating poetic beauty are defined, guṇas are seen to perform a function which is more important than merely adding verbal lustre to poetry (as alaNkaars do). The next logical step is to classify poetic beauty into two kinds.

Vaman does that by distinguishing between the 'natural' and 'artificial' beauty of poetry. Poetic beauty caused by guṇas has been called its 'natural' beauty, while alaNkaars create an 'artificial' or surface beauty in poetry. For the first kind of beauty, he uses the word 'shobhaa' and to describe the brightened and more attractive form of it, he used the term 'saundarya'. Thus, guṇas are responsible for the shobhaa of poetry while alaNkaars give it saundarya. Vaman, however, is not the first person to use the word 'shobhaa' to describe beauty in poetry. Almost a thousand years before him, Acharya Bharat had used the word to describe natural poetic beauty. Bharat uses the analogy of a beautiful woman who has natural graces or shobhaa which make her look attractive at all times. But if the same woman wears ornaments (alaNkaars) she will look even more beautiful. Bharat says that in the same manner, poetry should have a number of sahajaalaNkaars or natural graces such as shobhaa (beauty), maadhurya (sweetness), deepti (the ability to move and inspire) and so on. These elements give it a natural beauty. But when a poet uses alaNkaars such as an upamaa or a roopak the natural beauty of the poem is enhanced. Vaman thinks that poetic beauty is impossible without guṇas, while alaNkaars are optional.

Vaman goes on to explain the relationship between guṇas and reeti. For him, guṇas pertain to baNdha, which is a particular kind of organisation of the textual matter. We can also say that guṇas are generated when verse is organised in a particular fashion. Vaman says that oja, prasaad, shleSh, samataa, samaadhi, maadhurya, soukumaarya, udaarataa, arthavyakti and kaanti are the guṇas of the baNdhas, or poetic composition.

BaNdha can be of two kinds: shabdabaNdha and arthbaNdha. A shabdabaNdha is a specific kind of linguistic organisation while an arthbaNdha relates to the order in which content is presented. Vaman suggests that when a particular kind of baNdha is used, the poem acquires a certain guṇa or property. Similarly, when a baNdha is disturbed the guṇa disappears immediately. The realisation that there is a connection between baNdha and guṇa led Vaman to imagine the existence of some permanent source from which guṇas emerged. He concludes that guṇas have their potential being in reeti which is also the source of poetic beauty. He says that reeti is to poetry what the soul is to the body.

Thus, according to Vaman, the word and its sense constitute the body of poetry while reeti is its soul. Reeti is sometimes loosely translated as style or diction though it connotes much more than 'style'. It comes closer in meaning to 'rhythm' which is derived from the Greek root 'rheo' meaning 'to move' or 'to flow'.

MEANING OF REETI

Vaman defined reeti as,

> विशिष्ट पदरचना रीतिः। (*काव्यालंकारसूत्र*)
>
> vishiShta padrachanaa reetih | (*Kavyalankarsutra*)
>
> Reeti is a specific arrangement of padas.

According to the rules of Sanskrit grammar, we cannot use a word in the sentence; we need to use a pada, which is a word to which a vibhakti (suffix marking its grammatical function) has been added. Sanskrit grammar requires that a noun can be used in a sentence only if the marker (vibhakti) indicating its gender, person, number and case has been added to it. Only then does the word come to be called a pada. For example, 'Raam' is a word but 'Raamah' [Raam + visarga (:)] is a pada. When we use 'Raamah' in a sentence it indicates that it has masculine gender, is of singular number and is the subject of the verb. When Vaman uses the word 'padarachanaa' he means the order in which padas are arranged in a line of poetry.

According to Vaman, for a specific reeti to be produced, the padarachanaa must be vishiShTa. This means that to use a particular reeti a poet should compose his padas according to certain well-defined rules. These rules of composition are based on various kinds of combinations of words that go with a particular guṇa. Therefore, reeti and guṇa are interrelated.

We can understand it with the help of an example. Let us assume that a poet wants to describe a situation expressing the shriNgaar rasa. Now, the guṇa associated with shriNgaar rasa is maadhurya, that element in a poem which causes the heart to melt. For this guṇa to be present in a poem, the poet should not use long compound words (samaas) because long padas tends to work against this guṇa. For maadhurya guṇa the poet should use short padas (that is padas without samaas or the compounding of words) and only one certain set of consonants. In Chapter 3 we have seen the various requirements needed for achieving maadhurya guṇa in poetry. When the poet uses a style of composition which results in maadhurya guṇa, they would be using a particular reeti called the vaidarbhee reeti. This vaidarbhee reeti will help them in writing the kind of poetry that generates shriNgaar rasa. Thus, a particular reeti has to be used in order to achieve a particular guṇa which helps in the generation of a specific rasa. This is the correlation between reeti, guṇa and rasa.

It would be wrong, however, to think that padarachanaa and reeti are identical. If padarachanaa (the verbal structure) is the body of poetry, reeti is the soul that animates it. Therefore, vishiShTa padarachanaa is the verbal structure of the poem while reeti is the power behind it. Reeti is what that verbal structure is capable of suggesting in terms of its emotional meaning. VishiShTa padarachanaa is the medium through which the gunas become manifest and reveal the presence of reeti or the soul of poetry. Thus, reeti is the moving principle or directional force around which the gross (the language structure) and subtle (the network of meanings) bodies of poetry organise themselves. Reeti therefore determines the character of kaavya in the same manner as the soul determines the character of an individual. It is by virtue of reeti that the shabda shareer (a poem's gross body made of language) and artha shareer (a poem's subtle body made of its meaning) acquire shobhaa or beauty. We can also say that poetic beauty is nothing else but reeti in its vyakt (expressed) form.

While discussing the principle of reeti, Vaman introduces the term 'paak'. In its literal sense, 'paak' means 'being cooked'. In the context of poetry, it refers to that stage when poetry achieves maturity. The process by which poetry achieves maturity involves the appearance of guṇas in the texture of the gross and subtle bodies of poetry. The reason why guṇas appear in the texture of poetry is reeti and when it happens, guṇas and reeti blend into a single property. When this happens, the poem attains its paak, and it is this quality of paak which the sahridaya relishes.

Vaman envisions two kinds of paak—the shabdapaak and the arthapaak. The maturity of poetry comprises maturity in language use (shabdapaak) and maturity or profundity of meaning (arthapaak). Only that poetry is compellingly beautiful in which both these kinds of paaks blend into a single entity.

Vaman's concept of reeti is in consonance with the overall framework of Indian philosophy. The mainstream philosophies of India have a tradition of moving from diversity to unity. These philosophies consider the multiplicity of phenomena as perfectly valid and acceptable and yet also believe that behind all this heterogeneity of phenomena there is an ultimate reality principle that pervades this diversity. This model of 'many paths but one destination' is the framework for Vaman's theory of reeti. A number of elements need to coalesce to become good poetry and the principle that fuses all these elements into one body is reeti.

After Vaman, reeti as a concept continued to be discussed by scholars. Anandavardhan defines reeti in these words:

> संघटनस्वरूपमेव तवान्निरूप्यते। (*ध्वन्यालोक*)
>
> saNghaTanswaroopameva tavaanniroopyate | (*Dhwanyalok*)
>
> The organisation (of textual material) is the (outer) form of reeti.

Reeti for him is a certain kind of saNghaTan or the organisation of textual material. This organisation depends on particular guṇas and is a means of expressing the rasa. Kuntak says that the way the poet begins their journey is reeti. This statement brings the meaning of reeti much closer to that of diction. According to Kuntak the route a poet takes, that is, the diction they adopt to achieve their artistic ends, is what reeti is all about. In the fourteenth century, Vishwanath also said something similar and reiterated what Vaman had said:

> पदसंघटना रीतिरंग संस्थाविशेषवत् उपकर्त्री रसादिनाम्। (*साहित्यदर्पण*)
>
> padasaNghaTanaa reetiraNg saNsthaavisheShavat upakartree rasaadinaaM | (*Sahityadarpaṇ*)
>
> Like the proper arrangement of limbs in a person's body, reeti is a particular kind of arrangement of padas as a result of which rasas, et cetera, are intensified.

It is clear that by Vaman's time, the idea of reeti had received considerable attention and had been discussed at length. Reeti was seen as something more than verbal texture; it was an expression of a certain kind of poetic temperament. Vaman's contribution to Indian poetics is that he raises reeti from the level of poetic diction to the core, defining feature of poetry.

Table 7.1: Meaning of reeti

- Vaman, an eighth century Kashmiri scholar, propounded the theory of reeti.
- According to him, reeti is a special kind of organisation of textual material which includes organising both the language and the network of meanings. We can also say that reeti is a particular kind of style that a poet adopts.
- When a particular reeti is used, a certain kind of property or guṇa is generated in poetry.
- The emergence of that guṇa is the cause of the generation of a particular rasa, or creation of a certain state of mind.
- Since reeti is the original cause of the creation of rasa and is primarily responsible for poetic beauty, Vaman calls it 'the soul of poetry'.

KINDS OF REETI

Vaman discusses three kinds of reeti. Although these are named after the different geographical areas of ancient India, they are actually related to different kinds of diction, rhythm and sonority in poetry. The three reetis mentioned by Vaman are vaidarbhee, gauDee and paaNchaalee. Rudrat added a fourth reeti called laaTee. The word laaTee is related to 'LaaT', which is the old name of the present-day Gujarat. LaaTee is a mixture of vaidarbhee and paaNchaalee reetis.

It is necessary to remember that a poet is not always free to choose the reeti for his poem. More often than not, the choice of reeti is determined by the subject of the poem. For instance, if a poet wants to describe Krishna in a playful mood as a young man in Vrindavan, the description will look beautiful in the vaidarbhee reeti. But when the same Krishna is in the midst of the Mahabharata war, his description may require gauDee reeti. We shall now see what the features of these three reetis are.

Vaidarbhee Reeti

Vaman says that the vaidarbhee reeti has all the ten guṇas but is primarily associated with maadhurya guṇa. He considers this reeti to be ideal for all kinds of readers. Using the anthropomorphic analogy of kaavya, Vaman says that in the presence of the vaidarbhee reeti poetry appears to the reader as a very beautiful woman.

The vaidarbhee reeti is named after Vidarbha, which is the area around present-day Nagpur in Maharashtra. The most characteristic feature of this reeti is that the verse is mellifluous, soft and limpid, and flows easily. It is possible that when this reeti was identified with Vidarbha, it was seen as similar in sound to the sweet Prakrit that was spoken in that area and therefore, we can say that there is a possible link between this reeti and the tonal qualities of the language spoken by the people of Vidarbha.

The vaidarbhee reeti is related to a state of mind called druti. We have seen how poetry can produce different states of mind, one of which is druti. In this emotional state, the heart melts and the reader filled with tender feelings such as love or sorrow. This state of mind is produced by the maadhurya guṇa and, therefore, the vaidarbhee reeti is associated with this guṇa. Guṇas depend on the use of a particular kind of consonant, compound words and the subject on which the poem has been written.

When we consider the technical aspects of the vaidarbhee reeti, we note that sounds such as the hard /t/, hard /th/, hard /d/ and hard /dh/ are not permitted in this reeti. Secondly, most of the vowels used in this reeti have to be short. Thirdly, compound words (samaas) are either absent or used very sparingly. The net result of all this is that the verse becomes mellifluous and flows easily. The madhurya guṇa becomes manifest in this reeti which is primarily associated with karuṇ, shriNgaar (especially, viyog or separation of lovers) and shaaNta rasas.

GauDee Reeti

The vaidarbhi and gauDee reetis stand in sharp contrast. According to Dandin, the guṇas in gauDee reeti are the exact opposite of those in the vaidarbhee reeti. While vaidarbhee is limpid, mellifluous and smooth flowing, gauDee is ornate, elaborate and essentially baroque. In the gauDee reeti the verse has a majestic, rolling movement. We should remember that this reeti has been named after 'Gauda', which is the old name of Bengal. The literature of that area is known for its prominent display of the oja guṇa, that is, the expression of energy and power. It is clear, therefore, that the guṇa with which the gauDee reeti is most closely associated is oja.

The kings of the Pala dynasty, who ruled over Bengal and Bihar between the eighth and twelfth centuries, were great patrons of literature and benefactors of such famous universities as Nalanda and Vikramshila. They promoted literature in all languages including Sanskrit. In those days, the common languages in that area were Sanskrit and Prakrit, which included a proto-Bengali. This period is known as the late classical period of Sanskrit literature. The gauDee reeti developed during the rule of the Pala kings and, over the course of time, travelled to different parts of the country.

The gauDee reeti is associated with the oja guṇa. It is suitable for evoking the veer, raudra and vibhatsa rasas. This reeti creates a state of mind that is different from druti, which the vaidarbhee reeti engenders. While in druti the sahridaya's heart melts, in deepti and deeptivistaar his consciousness expands just like the blooming of the petals of a flower. The effect of the gauDee reeti is that the sahridaya experiences a surge of energy. It is this state of mind which is associated with the oja guṇa.

In the gaudee reeti, the hard /t/, hard /th/, hard /d/ and hard /dh/ sounds are prominently used. Compound words (samaas) can be used freely and can also be long. Rudrat says that gauDee is a kind of composition which has an abundance of long compound words—each compound word comprising seven or more words. This reeti is noted for its external splendour rather than its internal richness. When they needed it, even the greatest Sanskrit poets used gauDee reeti in their work. For instance, Kalidas—a poet famous for his preference for vaidarbhee reeti—has often used gauDee reeti.

PaNchaalee Reeti

Dandin uses the word 'maarg' for reeti and mentions only the vaidarbhee and gauDee maargs. Vaman uses the word 'reeti' for 'maarg' and adds a third reeti called paaNchaalee. This reeti is named after 'Panchal' which was the ancient name of North and Central India. In its rhythm, it is midway between the vaidarbhee and gauDee reetis.

The paaNchaalee reeti is associated chiefly with the prasaad guṇa though it also goes with the maadhurya and saukumarya (smoothness of the verse) guṇas. This reeti creates a state of mind that is different from both druti and deepti. We can describe this state of mind as simple happiness or prasaad. The mind is in a state which is midway between those called druti and deepti. This reeti does not make the heart melt nor does it make it expand as it happens in deepti or deeptivistaar. It is in a state of innocent joy with no evil or negative thoughts in it. Scholars have compared this state of mind with clear water. It is in this state of mind that prasaad guṇa is born, which is also present as an undercurrent in the other two states of mind.

In paaNchaalee reeti there is little use of compound words (samaas), although unlike vaidarbhee reeti (which does not favour long compound words at all), here the poet may use a few of them. This kind of writing style has an abundance of those words in which soft consonants are prominent. Words in which consonants such as /l/, /m/ and /n/ predominate are frequently used in paaNchaalee reeti. In this style of writing, words are generally short and are without elaborate alaNkaars. The rhythm in this reeti is graceful but can also be playful and bouncing. This reeti avoids the use of mahaapraaṇs (that is, the aspirated consonants located in the second and fourth places of the five clusters of consonants in the Devanagari alphabet, such as /kha/, /gha/, /chha/, /jha/ et cetera, and the three sibilants). It also avoids the use of nasal sounds (anuswar).

Table 7.2: Kinds of reeti

Kind of reeti	Guṇas associated with it	Characteristic features of the diction
vaidarbhee	all the ten guṇas but chiefly maadhurya	consonants such as the hard /t/, hard /th/, hard /d/ and hard /dh/ are avoided; vowels used are generally short; compound words (samaas) are either absent or used sparingly
gauDee	chiefly oja guṇa	consonants sounds such as the hard /t/, hard /th/, hard /d/ and hard /dh/ are prominently used; compound words (samaas) can be used freely and can also be long
paaNchaalee	prasaad guṇa	compound words used sparingly; abundance of soft consonants and free use of /l/, /m/ and /n/; short words without much alaNkaar; rhythm is graceful but sometimes playful also; no use of mahaapraaṇ consonants; absence of nasal sounds

For over a century, the school of Reeti enjoyed a place of prominence after which the Dhwani School appeared as its chief rival. Anandavardhan, the founder of the Dhwani School, praises Vaman very highly, although he also says that Vaman did not give the kind of importance to dhwani that he should have. Vaman's ideas about different kinds of diction continued to inspire later scholars. Rajshekhar went to the extent of calling the followers of the Reeti School, 'Vaamaniyaas' or 'the followers of Vaman'.

8

Dhwani

- Origin of the term
- Anandavardhan's theory of dhwani
- Definition of dhwani
- Two kinds of poetic meaning: vaachya and prateeyamaan
- Types of dhwani

The literal meaning of dhwani is 'sound' or 'resonance'. In Sanskrit literary theory, the term signifies those subtle nuances of meaning that poetry is capable of conveying. Fundamentally, the theory of dhwani is concerned with semantics. When we read a poem, it often happens that we discover different layers of meaning in it. The poem has a literal meaning; but if it is more than just 'verse' it also has a figurative and symbolic meaning. That figurative and symbolic meaning is not evident on the surface but, when we read the poem carefully, we become aware of it. That deeper meaning is the 'dhwani' of that poem. We can also say that when a poem 'sounds' different from what it says on the surface, it has the quality of dhwani in it. In other words, when a poem has the ability to resonate with complex themes and emotions it is an example of dhwani kaavya or poetry which has dhwani.

Origin of the Term

The term 'dhwani' was first used in Sanskrit grammar, from where it was borrowed by scholars of Indian poetics. Dhwani as a concept is related to the idea of sphoTa, a term used by grammarians while discussing semantics. In order to explain the process by which a word conveys its meaning, Sanskrit grammarians came up with the theory of sphoTa. This theory is specifically associated with the name of Bhartrihari, a Sanskrit poet and grammarian of the fifth century CE. In his *Vakyapadiyam* he discusses the concept of sphoTa, though even before him grammarians like Panini and Patanjali had mentioned it.

The word sphoTa has been derived from 'sphuT' which means 'to bloom' or 'to burst'. The theory tries to explain the process by which words convey their meaning. Simply stated, the theory says that when we hear the different phonemes of a word being spoken the meaning of the word 'bursts forth' only after we have heard the last phoneme. This happens because of sphoTa which, according to Dr S. Radhakrishnan (*The Principal Upanishads*), is the indivisible idea with its dual forms of shabda (word) and artha (meaning). When we pronounce a word, we actually pronounce the different phonemes that it is made up of. As soon as a phoneme is pronounced, the one uttered just before it is destroyed. This continues till we reach the last phoneme of the word. Then the question is: When all the phonemes uttered before the last phoneme are destroyed, how is it that we still understand the meaning of what has been said? The answer given by Sanskrit grammar is that each pronounced phoneme of a word reveals its sphoTa bit by bit. Of course, the first phoneme reveals it only vaguely and all the subsequently pronounced phonemes make it progressively clear, till the last phoneme is uttered and the meaning of the word is revealed to us. Thus, grammarians see a word as having two aspects: sphoTa and dhwani. SphoTa is the permanent, indivisible and indestructible element of the word while dhwani is its actualised form. It means that sphoTa is the concept whereas dhwani is the enunciated word expressing that concept. It is in this sense that while the spoken word is ephemeral, the concept is permanently present in the mind of the user of the language.

Dhwani can have no meaning without sphoTa. Different people may pronounce a word differently, but the linguistic value of that word is the same for everyone because the word is related to the same unchanging sphoTa, which is the proto word. In course of time, grammarians began to use the word 'dhwani' to denote the manifest form of sphoTa. On this basis, Anandavardhan and other scholars of the Dhwani School began to use dhwani for the suggested meaning (prateeyamaan artha) of kaavya. Thus, his theory of dhwani is based on the concept of sphoTa. As individual phonemes used independently are unable to express the meaning of a word, in poetry its literal and indicative meanings cannot reveal its entire beauty. That beauty is revealed only through its dhwani, that is, its suggested and symbolic meaning.

ANANDAVARDHAN'S THEORY OF DHWANI

Anandavardhan is the principal exponent of the theory of dhwani. His *Dhwanyalok* ('The light of dhwani'), a book written in the ninth century, is the primary text on this theory. However, it would be incorrect to believe that he was the first to use this term, or that the concept of dhwani was unknown before him. His great contribution is that he established dhwani as the central element of poetry. After him, dhwani became one of the core criteria for assessing the quality of poetry. Anandavardhan's *Dhwanyalok* begins with these words:

> काव्यस्यात्मा ध्वनिरिति बुधैर्यः समाम्नातपूर्वः । (ध्वन्यालोक)
>
> kaavyasyaatmaa dhwaniriti budhairyah samaamnaatpoorvah ।
> (*Dhwanyalok*)
>
> Dhwani, which was mentioned and accepted by scholars before me, is the soul or fundamental element of poetry.

The rest of the book elaborates the idea that dhwani is the soul of poetry. By the 'soul of poetry' Anandavardhan means that aspect of poetry without which poetry loses its special character. It is the element that separates poetry from non-poetry. Poetry is different from other kinds of writing because it has a special kind of meaning which is different from its literal (abhidhaa) or indicated (lakShaṇaa) meaning. It has dhwani or vyaNgyaarth which enables it to convey much more than the surface meaning of the words used in it. After mentioning and evaluating different kinds of poetry, Anandavardhan asserts that only that poetry which has dhwani or vyaNgyaarth can be called real poetry. He says that, in actual fact there is only one kind of poetry and that is dhwani kaavya.

To formulate his theory of dhwani, Anandavardhan considers a fundamental question: how do words convey their meaning? He says that words have two kinds of powers with whose help they convey meaning. He calls these powers mukhya (primary) and amukhya (non-primary). The primary word power is abhidhaa which gives the literal meaning of the word. The non-primary word power is of two kinds: lakShaṇaa (which gives the indicated meaning of the word) and vyaNjanaa (which conveys its suggested meaning). We have seen the difference between abhidhaa, lakShaṇaa and vyaNjanaa in Chapter 4.

Anandavardhan emphasises the role of vyaNjanaa in poetry and considers it the central element of poetry. Dhwani is the meaning conveyed by a poem's vyaṇjanaa power and it is this kind of meaning that distinguishes poetry from other kinds of writing. Anandavardhan constructed his theory of dhwani around this core idea. In later times also, this theory continued to receive the attention of scholars which is evident from the fact that a very large number of commentaries were written on *Dhwanyalok*, of which Abhinavagupt's *Dhwanyaloklochan* is certainly the most important.

Definition of Dhwani

Defining dhwani, Anandavardhan says that when both the literal expression and its literal meaning are given less importance than what they suggest or imply, it is called dhwani. He writes,

> यत्रार्थः शब्दो वा तमर्थमुपसर्जनीकृतस्वार्थौ,
> व्यङ्क्तः काव्यविशेषः स ध्वनिरिति सुरिभिः कथितः। (ध्वन्यालोक)
>
> yatraarthah shabdo vaa tamarthmupsarjaneekrit swaarthau,
> vyaNktah kaavyavisheShah sa dhwaniriti suribhih kathitah ।
> (*Dhwanyalok*)
>
> Where the vaachak (literal expression) and vaachya (its literal meaning) make themselves and their meaning secondary and express their symbolic meaning, scholars call it dhwani.

The theory of dhwani is based on the principle that the ultimate aim of poetry is not to state its literal meaning but to convey a deeper implicit sense. Only such poetry can be called truly beautiful. Applying this principle to poetry, Anandavardhan declares that dhwani kaavya or poetry in which dhwani predominates is the finest kind (uttam) of poetry.

Anandavardhan illustrates the meaning of dhwani with the help of an example. A woman used to meet her lover at a secret place on the banks of the Godavari River. There was a forest on both sides of the river. A sadhu (ascetic) also went there to bathe in the river. The woman did not like the sadhu visiting that place because she met her lover there. There was a dog in the forest which always barked at the sadhu when he came to bathe in the river. One day, the woman said to the sadhu, 'O Sadhu, now you can come to this place without any fear of the dog because the dog which barked at you has now been killed by an angry lion which lives in the forests of the Godavari'. The literal meaning (vaachyaarth) of this statement is that now it is safe for the sadhu to come to the banks of the Godavari because the dog that troubled him has been killed by the lion. But the dhwani (vyaNgyaarth) of this statement is the exact opposite of its literal meaning or vaachyaarth. She is actually telling the ascetic, 'It is not at all safe for you to come to this place because although the dog has been killed, in its place there is an angry lion here which will kill you and eat you'. According to Anandavardhan, it is the dhwani or the suggested meaning of a statement which is its real meaning.

Anandavardhan says that poetry can be written in many forms, but all its forms have one thing in common and that is dhwani. He goes on to say that if there is no dhwani in poetry, it is not poetry at all. Dhwani therefore is the aatmaa or soul of poetry which gives it meaning and which distinguishes it from all other kinds of writing.

Almost a century after it was written, another Kashmiri scholar named Abhinavagupt wrote a commentary on *Dhwanyalok* and called his book *Dhwanyaloklochan*. He reiterates and explains Anandavardhan's concept of dhwani and says that the ultimate goal of suggestion (dhwani) is the generation of rasa. He further says that those scholars who consider beauty to be the essence of poetry are also correct because in a fundamental sense, there is no difference between dhwani and poetic beauty.

TWO KINDS OF POETIC MEANING: VAACHYA AND PRATEEYAMAAN

Anandavardhan says that there can be two kinds of poetic meaning: vaachya and prateeyamaan. He further says that since earlier acharyas have already discussed the first kind of meaning (vaachya) in great detail, he will focus only on the prateeyamaan artha. The fundamental difference between vaachya and prateeyamaan meaning is that in a poem, the vaachya meaning is conveyed with the help of its language (which may or may not have poetic figures or alaNkaars), but its prateeyamaan artha is conveyed by the beauty of the entire poem. This is to say that we cannot single out an element in the poem and say that this particular element is the cause of its charm. Poetry in which the prateeyamaan meaning predominates is called dhwani kaavya.

Explaining further the meaning of prateeyamaan artha, Anandavardhan writes:

> प्रतीयमानं पुनरन्यदेव वस्त्वस्ति वाणीषु महाकवीनाम्,
> यत् तत् प्रसिद्धावयवातिरिक्तं विभाति लावण्यमिवांगनासु। (*ध्वन्यालोक*)
>
> prateeyamaanaM punaranyadeva vastvasti vaaṇeeShu mahaakaveenam,
> yat tat prasiddhaavayavaatiriktam vibhaati laavaṇyamivaaNganaasu |
> (*Dhwanyalok*)
>
> Prateeyamaan is different from the beauty of various parts of a woman's body; it is the loveliness of the whole and much more. It is that beauty which is felt in its entirety; which dwells deeper and beyond the meanings of the verses of the great scholars and poets.

In these lines Anandavardhan uses an analogy to explain the difference between the vaachyaarth and the prateeyamaan artha of a poem. He says that the laavaṇya or loveliness of a woman is not separate from the beauty of the various parts of her body and yet it is something more than the sum total of the beauty of the parts of her body. That laavaṇya is something mysteriously charming. In the same manner, the voice (poetry) of great poets has a prateeyamaan artha which is different from the literal meaning of their words and that is the reason why their poetry appears so wonderful. Anandavardhan thus suggests that elements of poetry such as alaNkaar, guṇa and others are like the face and limbs of a beautiful woman but the prateeyamaan artha is like her beauty (laavaṇya) itself which is much more than the beauty of her body. The prateeyamaan artha cannot be explained in words; it can only be experienced.

According to Anandavardhan, the level of greatness of a poet is determined by his ability to write poetry which has a suggested or prateeyamaan meaning. Only a poet endowed with pratibhaa (natural talent) can comprehend and convey the prateeyamaan artha of poetry. That is the reason why the writing of all great poets have this element of dhwani which is the potential to suggest much more that what the poem has to say on the surface. Anandavardhan's theory of dhwani, therefore, subsumes stylistic elements of poetry such as alaNkaar, reeti and guṇas under the overarching concept of dhwani.

TYPES OF DHWANI

Anandavardhan has classified dhwani into multiple types and subtypes. He makes this classification on the basis of the three different kinds of shabdashakti or word power. We know that words have three different kinds of power, or modes of signification: abhidhaa, lakShaṇaa and vyaNjanaa. When a word gives its meaning in its abhidhaa mode, we understand its literal meaning, that is, its common dictionary meaning. This meaning is the same for everyone. When a word conveys its meaning in the lakShaṇaa mode we understand it in a sense which is different from its literal meaning, although related to it. This kind of meaning too might be the same for everyone. But when a word displays its vyaNjanaa shabdashakti, we understand it in a sense that is different from both its literal and indicated meanings. On the basis of these different kinds of shabdashakti, dhwani has been categorised into three broad classes: abhidhaamooladhwani, lakShaṇaamooladhwani and vyaNjanaadhwani.

Abhidhaamooladhwani

When the suggested meaning of an expression is based on the abhidhaa or literal meaning of the words used in it, it is known as abhidhaamooladhwani where 'abhidhaa' means 'literal' and 'moola' means 'rooted in'. It is also known as shaabdivyaNjanaa. If a poet uses a word which has two different literal meanings and both of which make sense, it is an example of abhidhaamooladhwani. Here dhwani is created by the polysemous nature of the words used.

To take an example, in Shakespeare's play *Romeo and Juliet*, Mercutio, bleeding to death, says,

> Ask for me tomorrow and you shall find me a grave man.
>
> (*Romeo and Juliet*, Act III Scene 1, William Shakespeare)

Here the expression 'grave man' can be understood in two senses: first, 'a serious man' and secondly, a 'man in the grave' that is, 'a dead man'. In the context of the play, Mercutio is saying that by tomorrow he will be dead. Since both the meanings are literal, it is an example of abhidhaamooladhwani.

LakShaṇaamooladhwani

LakShaṇaamoola means 'rooted in the lakShaṇaa' ('mool' means 'root'). In this kind of dhwani, the suggested meaning is based not on the literal but the indicated meaning of a word. We cannot understand the real meaning of this kind of statement if we take it in its literal sense only. We have to consider the indicated meaning of the words used. To take an example:

> सुवर्णपुष्पां पृथिवीं चिन्वन्ति पुरुषस्त्रयः,
> शूरश्च कृतविद्यश्च यश्च जानाति सेवितुम्। (*ध्वन्यालोक*)
>
> suvarṇapuShpaaM prithiveeM chinvanti puruShastrayah,
> shoorashcha kritavidyashcha yashcha jaanaati sevitum |
>
> (*Dhwanyalok*)
>
> This earth on which flowers of gold bloom can be possessed only by three kinds of men: those who are brave, those who are scholars and those who know how to serve.

Now, the earth is not a tree or a creeper on which we can find flowers of gold. So, the indicated meaning of 'flowers of gold' is 'worldly goods' or 'property'. Material goods, therefore, are the 'flowers of gold' which bloom in this world. Thus, the dhwani of these lines is that only people with courage ('brave'), intellect and knowledge ('scholars') and the willingness to serve others can acquire wealth in this world.

We can understand lakShaṇaamooladhwani with the help of another example. If someone says, 'He is Kumbhakarna' we cannot take the statement at its face value because the person spoken of is neither the brother of Ravana, the king of Lanka, nor are his ears big like pots ('Kumbhakarna' literally means 'a person whose ears are large like hanging pots'). This statement can only have an indicated meaning. It means that person referred to is very fond of eating and sleeping, and these are the attributes he shares with Kumbhakarna, Ravana's brother in the Ramayana. Here the dhwani is that the speaker expects nothing from the person they are talking about. They call him 'Kumbhakarna' to suggest that this person is extremely lazy and therefore he cannot be given any responsibility. Since this kind of dhwani or suggested meaning is based on the lakShaṇaa mode of the word, we call it lakShaṇaamooladhwani.

VyaNjanaadhwani

When an expression has vyaNjanaadhwani it conveys to us a suggested or symbolic meaning which we are able to understand only when we have understood the context in which the expression has been used. This suggested meaning may not be the same for everyone. This kind of dhwani belongs to the domain of the vyaNjanaa shabdashakti.

We can understand vyaNjanaadhwani with the help of an example. Let us take the following lines from John Keats' *Ode to a Nightingale*:

Fade far away, dissolve, and quite forget
    What thou among the leaves hast never known,
The weariness, the fever, and the fret
    Here, where men sit and hear each other groan;

Where palsy shakes a few, sad, last gray hairs,
Where youth grows pale, and spectre-thin, and dies;
Where but to think is to be full of sorrow
And leaden-eyed despairs,
Where Beauty cannot keep her lustrous eyes,
Or new Love pine at them beyond to-morrow.
(*Ode to a Nightingale*, John Keats)

These lines, as we know, are addressed to the nightingale which sings as if it has never known what men and women living in this world have to know. He mentions a number of unhappy things that every person in this world has to experience, whether young or old, ordinary or beautiful. But the dhwani of the poem has a much wider context and a sensitive reader will be able to see, feel and experience much more than what the poem says on the surface. And every reader of Keats' poem will have a slightly different experience of it, that is, its dhwani will be different for different readers.

Vastudhwani, AlaNkaardhwani and Rasadhwani

Anandavardhan offers another classification of dhwani. There can be three kinds of dhwani according to this classification. These are vastudhwani, alaNkaardhwani and rasadhwani. Vastudhwani is the suggested meaning of an expression that has no alaNkaars. AlaNkaardhwani is the implicit meaning of an expression in which there is an alaNkaar or figure of speech. But rasadhwani is that expression which is capable of evoking emotion. Because it evokes emotion, it helps in the generation of a rasa. Anandavardhan has called rasadhwani the very soul of poetry. It is also the finest kind of poetry.

Anandavardhan says that if a single piece of poetry generates multiple rasas, the chief rasa among them is the rasadhwani of that poem and the other rasas are secondary and are known as rasavaadalaNkaar. The suggested meaning of the first two kinds of dhwani can be expressed in language but the emotion evoked by rasadhwani cannot be described in words. Because it is a feeling, it can only be experienced.

Table 8.1: Types of Dhwani

Type of dhwani	Feature
abhidhaamooladhwani	the suggested sense of an expression which has a word with two different literal meanings both of which make sense in the expression
lakShaṇaamooladhwani	is based on the indicated or figurative sense of a word used in it
vyaNjanaadhwani	the suggested or symbolic meaning of an expression which is understood only when the context in which the expression has been used is also understood
vastudhwani	the suggested meaning of an expression in which no figure of speech has been used
alaNkaardhwani	the suggested meaning of an expression in which a figure of speech has been used and that poetic figure is the source of the implied sense of the expression
rasadhwani	the emotion evoked by an expression

The school of Dhwani is considered so important that the entire history of Indian poetics is divided into three periods: pre-dhwani, dhwanikaal (the age of dhwani) and post-dhwani periods. Bhamah, Dandin, Udbhat, Vaman and Rudrat belong to the pre-dhwani age in which the AlaNkaar School predominates. In the age of dhwani, to which Anandavardhan, Kuntak and Mahim Bhatt belong, the prateeyamaan artha or internal beauty of kaavya was given more importance than alaNkaar. And finally, we have the post-dhwani period which witnessed new dimensions of dhwani being explored by scholars such as Mammat, Ruyyak, Vidyadhar, Vishwanath, Jagannath and others, and at the same time there were scholars like Jaydev, Keshav Mishra and Appaya Diskshit who sought to revive the ideas and style of the pre-dhwani age.

9

Vakrokti

- The meaning of vakrokti
- Kuntak's theory of vakrokti
- Kinds of vakrokti

THE MEANING OF VAKROKTI

Vakrokti is made up of two words: 'vakra' (not straight) and 'ukti' (utterance). The word therefore means 'an oblique utterance'. Before Rajanak Kuntak, who lived in the tenth century CE, the word was used to denote hyperbole. Kuntak provided a larger context to the term and raised it to the level of an independent literary theory. This theory makes a clear distinction between non-literary and literary language. Kuntak uses the term vakrokti to describe literary language which is different from ordinary, day-to-day conversation. The term also describes a particular kind of writing strategy which poets use in order to produce a text that can please the reader. That text, or poetry, is characterised by euphony, wit, inventiveness and dexterity of expression. But we should not imagine that vakrokti is merely a display of the poet's linguistic brilliance. It is closer in meaning to their creative imagination which can transform something ordinary into exquisite poetry. We shall have more to say about it later.

As we have seen, the theory of vakrokti is associated with the name of Rajanak Kuntak. He was a Kashmiri scholar of the tenth century CE and was one of the most respected writers of his time. This is evident from the title 'Rajanak' before his name. It was a title given by the kings of Kashmir to the greatest scholars of their time. We are fairly certain about the time in which he lived because we know the periods of some of those writers whom he has quoted. For example, he has quoted profusely from Rajshekhar's works and Anandavardhan's *Dhwanyalok* which indicates that he must have lived after 900CE. But he has not quoted from any work of Abhinavagupt whose literary career spans from around 980 to 1020CE. We also know that Mahim Bhatt, who lived in the eleventh century, has written a critique of Kuntak's theory. All these facts tell us that Kuntak must have lived in the middle of the tenth century.

By the middle of the tenth century, when Kuntak wrote his *Vakroktijeevit*, the then dominant theory of alaNkaar had almost run its course. A few decades before him, Anandavardhan had already changed the direction of academic discourse by highlighting the importance of rasa and dhwani. This implies that alaNkaar no longer enjoyed the prominence it once did. It was at this time that Kuntak appeared on the scene and put forward his theory of vakrokti which provided an entirely new method of evaluating poetry. He declared that vakrokti is the life (jeev) of poetry. It meant that all other elements of poetry, such as alaNkaars (figures of speech), dhwani (a poem's ability to suggest more than it says) and rasa (the emotional impact poetry has on the reader), were pushed to second place and only vakrokti was central to it.

Kuntak chose the term vakrokti to express his concept of literary style. It was not a new term and before him it only meant hyperbole. Yet, it is also a fact that it was considered one of the most important alaNkaars (figures of speech) by earlier scholars. Kuntak gave another meaning to the term. At the very beginning of his *Vakroktijeevit* he declares that his intention in the book is to establish the validity of his theory about the relationship between poetic beauty (which he calls chamatkaar or a 'miracle') and literary language. He says that he has written this book in order to establish a new idea, which has not been discussed before. He further says that a striking poetic expression is the cause of chamatkaar in poetry. By chamatkaar he means a miracle, or the sense of wonder which poetry creates in the reader.

At this stage, it would be useful to take a brief look at the history of the term vakrokti. It was first used by Bhamah in the sixth century CE to denote hyperbole. He, however, also says that it is no ordinary figure of speech and believes that a poet cannot hope to achieve poetic beauty without using vakrokti in their writing. He even goes to the extent of saying that a poem without vakrokti is not a poem at all, but merely a statement.

In the next century, Dandin also commented on vakrokti. He says that poetry can be classified into two groups: swabhaavokti and vakrokti. Swabhaavokti has two meanings: first, it means an expression that is natural and spontaneous; and secondly, it also means describing something exactly as it is. This is to say that there cannot be any figures of speech in swabhaavokti. Vakrokti, on the other hand, is the exact opposite of swabhaavokti. It is anything but a plain and objective statement. It is often oblique and describes something in a 'poetic' manner, that is, it makes use of various poetic devices such as metaphors, similes, and so on. The most easily recognisable feature of vakrokti is that it has a tendency to exaggerate a description. Dandin says that vakrokti lends vaichitriya to poetry. In other words, it makes the description of something look vichitra or strange and unfamiliar, and therefore, striking. But he also cautions us when he says that every piece of eccentric and strange-looking writing is not vakrokti. There is a difference between a curious and odd expression and genuine poetry, of which vakrokti is an element. Dandin says that poetry should be 'tadvidaahlaadakari'. It means that it must have the ability to 'give immediate pleasure to the reader'. So, he says that vakrokti is an alaNkaar (a figure of speech) which contributes to the enjoyment of the reader. He also adds that it is the most important alaNkaar.

In the eighth century, we have Vaman who also considers vakrokti as an alaNkaar. But he expands the scope of the term and includes the lakShaṇaa shabdashakti in it. In the chapter on shabdashakti (the potential of a word to convey its meaning), we have come across the word lakShaṇaa. It simply refers to that power of the word which enables it to convey an indicated meaning, which is different from its literal meaning although related to it. We also recall that when a word is used in its literal sense, it is said to be expressing its abhidhaa power. We can understand the difference between abhidhaa and lakShaṇaa with the help of an example.

If someone says, 'This is a donkey', we understand the word 'donkey' in its literal sense and therefore it is in abhidhaa. But if they say, 'You are a donkey' we understand the word 'donkey' in its indicated sense. Here the indicated meaning of 'donkey' is to tell the person that they have the same attributes as a donkey, that is, they are dull-headed and stupid. In this sentence, the word 'donkey' has been used in lakShaṇaa, or in its indicated sense. When a word is used in lakShaṇaa, we first become aware of its primary or literal meaning and then reject it in favour of some other indicated meaning depending on the context in which it has been used. Vaman says that lakShaṇaa also is a kind of vakrokti.

In the ninth century, Anandavardhan equated vakrokti with hyperbole and said that all alaNkaars have the basic tendency to lean towards vakrokti. After him, other scholars such as Rudrat and Abhinavagupt also accepted the definition of vakrokti given by Bhamah. It was at this stage that Kuntak asserted that vakrokti is not only a rhetorical device but the core defining feature of poetry.

KUNTAK'S THEORY OF VAKROKTI

Kuntak discusses his theory of vakrokti in his *Vakroktijeevit*, a seminal text from which later scholars have quoted profusely. The book is divided into four chapters, each called an unmeSh. Each chapter has kaarikaas (memorial verses), vrittis (explanations) and udaaharaṇs (examples). The kaarikaas and vrittis are written by Kuntak but almost all the examples have been taken from other writers. The first chapter deals with topics such as the definition of poetry, its characteristics, its purpose, and then introduces six kinds of vakrokti. The second chapter discusses in detail three of these six vakroktis, namely, varṇavinyaasavakrataa, padapoorvaardhavakrataa and padottaraardhavakrataa. In the third chapter vaakyavakrataa and alaNkaars have been dealt with. In the final chapter, prakaraṇvakrataa and prabaNdhavakrataa have been explained.

Kuntak begins by declaring that vakrokti is the core defining feature of poetry. It means that no poetry is possible without vakrokti. He writes,

वक्रोक्तिः काव्यजीवितम्। (*वक्रोक्तिजीवित*)

vakroktih kaavyajeevitam | (*Vakroktijeevit*)

Vakrokti is the breathful life (praaṇabhoota tattva) of poetry.

He believes that for all kinds of poetry, vakrokti is as important as the flow of breath (praaṇ) is for a living being. He does not deny the importance of dhwani in poetry but feels that it can be subsumed under the broad category of vakrokti. Vakrokti is the praaṇ (the flow of breath) of poetry while dhwani is its soul. The difference between breath and soul is the difference between vakrokti and dhwani. The togetherness of the soul and the body is possible only until a person has praaṇ or breath in their body. In poetry, that praaṇ is vakrokti.

In the sixth century CE, Bhamah considered vakrokti as the root of all alaNkaars ('sarvaalaNkaarmoola'). Kuntak further explores this and raises the concept into an independent poetic theory in the tenth century, yet his poetic explorations and achievements were properly accepted and appreciated only in the fourteenth century by Vishwanath. Many critics of Kuntak often miss this point when they say that he completely rejected Anandavardhan's theory of dhwani in favour of vakrokti. After having established the centrality of vakrokti in poetry, he goes on to define poetry from this standpoint:

कवेः कर्म काव्यम्। (*वक्रोक्तिजीवित*)

kaveh karma kaavyaM | (*Vakroktijeevit*)

Poetry is what the poet does.

He further says,

तदुपायतया तत्वं सालंकारस्य काव्यता। (*वक्रोक्तिजीवित*)

tadupaayatayaa tatvaM saalaNkaarasya kaavyataa | (*Vakroktijeevit*)

AlaNkaar is an essential part of poetry.

And then adds:

शब्दार्थौ सहितौ वक्रकविव्यापारशालिनि,
बन्धे व्यवस्थितौ काव्यं तद्विदाह्लादकारिणि। (*वक्रोक्तिजीवित*)

shabdaarthau sahitau vakrakavivyaapaarashaalini,
bandhe vyavasthitau kaavyaM tadvidaahlaadakariṇi | (*Vakroktijeevit*)

> Poetry is that strikingly beautiful (vakra) composition (baNdha) in which words and meanings are organised according to a particular order, which gives aesthetic pleasure (to the reader).

In his definition, Kuntak makes certain important points about poetry. First of all, he says that kaavya is what the kavi produces. Then, who is a kavi? As we saw in the introductory chapter, a kavi or a poet has been regarded as a person gifted with special abilities such as having the skill to express thoughts and feelings in a striking language. When Kuntak says that kaavya is the work of a kavi, he is implying that since an exceptionally gifted person creates it, it is something precious and not commonly found.

After having established the preciousness of kaavya, Kuntak says that alaNkaars are an essential part of it. It means, that language which has been embellished (alaNkrit) by figures of speech is the material form, or the body, of poetry. After showing how language or composition is the body of poetry, Kuntak defines vakrokti in the verse quoted above.

According to this definition, poetry is composition that is vakra (oblique). The term 'vakra' suggests that the language of poetry is not the language which people use in their daily lives. Thus, he draws a clear distinction between poetic diction and ordinary speech. Poetic diction is not only different from ordinary speech but also transcends it. The adjective 'vakra' therefore denotes the features of this special kind of language which poets use for writing poetry. These features include qualities such as the language being inspired, striking, witty, and so on.

The next point Kuntak makes in his definition is that poetry is fundamentally baNdha or composition. BaNdha refers to the order in which words and their denotative and connotative meanings are organised. In order to be called poetry, this organisation must be of a special kind. But this special kind of organisation of material must be able to give immediate pleasure to the reader. Thus, Kuntak says four things: first, poetry is the work of a person (kavi) who knows a great deal about the world and who also has the skill to describe something well. Secondly, its language is not what we use in our daily lives; it is embellished by alaNkaars. Thirdly, it is a special kind of composition characterised by an obliquity of expression. And finally, it can give joy to the reader. The term vakrokti as used by Kuntak contains all these ideas. We can say that vakrokti is a striking mode of speech which is capable of pleasing the reader.

Kuntak illustrates his concept of vakrokti by quoting a verse from Kalidas' *Meghdoot*. We know that *Meghdoot* is one of the most famous long poems of Kalidas which, in one hundred and fifteen stanzas, tells the story of a yakSh in exile. In Hindu, Jain and Buddhist mythology, yakShaas are a class of nature spirits who take care of natural treasures hidden in the earth and in the roots of trees. They are generally benevolent but may also be evil. In the poem by Kalidas, the narrator is a yakSh who is a subject of Kuber, the king of yakShs and the Hindu god of wealth. He has been punished by the god for neglecting his duties and has been exiled for one year to central India. He is alone and pining for his wife who is in Alakapuri on Mount Kailash in the Himalayas. He is able to convince a passing cloud to take his message of love to his wife. He describes to the cloud all the beautiful things it will see during its journey from central India to the Himalayas. When the cloud reaches Alakapuri, the yakSh wants it to wake his wife gently if she is sleeping, in the same manner as the maalati flowers are revived when the rains come. And then, he wants the cloud to say these words to her,

> You see me as a cloud. I am a bosom friend of your dear loved one who wants you to hear his message treasured in my heart. You know, I am the one who, speaking in low and pleasant rumblings, drives the lagging travellers on the road to their women who are pining for them, the travellers who have eager thoughts of unbinding the hair (veṇi) of their loved women.
>
> (*Meghdoot*, Uttarmegh, verse 36, Kalidas)

Kuntak finds this verse a perfect example of vakrokti. In the beginning of the verse itself, he says, we come across the word 'friend', which creates a sense of confidence in the mind of the person being addressed. The fact that the cloud is her husband's friend suggests that it is respectable and therefore, can be believed. The closeness of this friendship is reinforced further by the word 'bosom' which strengthens the possibility of the cloud having been entrusted with a confidential message. Having thus won her confidence, the cloud comes to the point of the message. The expression 'treasured in my heart' reveals his keenness to preserve this precious message. Kuntak asks: one may wonder why someone else with better understanding and talent was not chosen to deliver this message? The answer is provided by the cloud himself. The cloud suggests that only he has the qualifications for delivering a message of this kind. He is the natural carrier of water, and therefore carrying precious things is his basic nature. Again, he also has the ability to send tired travellers tarrying on the road to their beloved women by speaking to them in a low and rumbling voice. The sweet and pleasing sounds made by the cloud show that he knows how an ideal messenger should speak. It is his nature to unite lovers.

Kuntak further says that the use of the plural number in this verse implies how the cloud helps everyone in the world. The reference to 'lagging travellers' on the road indicates the cloud's tendency to help even those who are not related to him. The idea behind the verse is that it is the chosen mission of the cloud to show his friendship to man by uniting lovers. The lines express the beautiful thought that love pervades all of creation. This thought expresses the essence of the entire poem which has rightly been called *Meghdoot* or the 'Cloud messenger'. This beautiful thought has been expressed in mellifluous words and therefore this is vakrokti of the finest kind, which brings great joy to the cultivated reader.

We see that Kuntak's definition of vakrokti is different from that given by scholars before him. It is clear that he does not consider it an alaNkaar but a term for fine poetry itself. He says that when a thing or condition is expressed indirectly, or in a vichitra manner, it is called vakrokti. He calls vakrokti 'vaichitraabhidhaa' (a striking denotation). It is the element of vaichitriya (having the qualities of strangeness, novelty and beauty at the same time) that is responsible for the extraordinary charm of poetry. But he also adds that this principle of vakrokti applies both to words and meaning. Neither beautiful language nor impressive content in itself can result in poetry. He believes that when a poet says something ordinary in a beautiful and musical language, the poet is displaying the poverty of their imagination, that is, the daaridriya (poverty) of their pratibhaa (imagination), as he puts it. Similarly, a striking idea expressed in a banal language is also not poetry.

KINDS OF VAKROKTI

Kuntak identifies six kinds of vakrokti. The poet has multiple options of arranging their material in such a way that they achieve the effect they want. The poet can begin by organising the consonant sounds in a line. They can move one step further and pay attention to arranging the words in a sentence. They can also try to arrange their sentences in a particular order. The different sections of a long poem can also be arranged in a striking manner. And finally, the poet can even experiment with the genre itself. All these manipulations with material are examples of vakrokti. Now we shall look at these six kinds of vakrokti in some detail.

Varṇavinyaasavakrataa

Varṇavinyaasavakrataa means the arrangement (vinyaas) of varṇas (phonemes) in a vakra (striking) manner. The result of such arrangement is vaichitriya (the quality of being striking). What Kuntak insists on is that there must be perfect harmony between sound and sense in poetry. He identifies three kinds of varṇavinyaasavakrataa:

1. repetition of one consonant
2. repetition of two consonants
3. repetition of more than two consonants.

Kuntak admits that the idea of varṇavinyaas is not something new and says that it was known by another name in the past. He says that varṇavinyaasavakrataa was known to ancient scholars also but as anupraas or alliteration. However, according to him varṇavinyaasavakrata, or sound-sequencing, is a much more complex element than anupraas. For proper varṇavinyaasavakrataa to occur, a few conditions must be fulfilled

First, a poet cannot use consonant sounds in an arbitrary manner. These sounds should be appropriate to the subject they are writing about. The poet has to ensure that the sound of the words they are using does not dilute the emotional impact of the poem.

Secondly, the repetition of a consonant sound should not look contrived and laboured. The poem should not give the impression that the poet has planned the arrangement of sounds too carefully. Kuntak believes that there should be a spontaneous quality in the flow of the verse.

Thirdly, varṇavinyaasavakrataa should not result in monotony of sound. There should be enough variety and novelty in it to please the reader.

Fourthly, in trying to achieve varṇavinyaasavakrataa the poet should ensure the presence of the prasaad guṇa throughout the composition. In other words, to achieving a particular sound effect, the poet cannot sacrifice qualities like lucidity and spontaneity in poetry.

Finally, Kuntak says that whatever be the kind of varṇavinyaasavakrataa, the poem should always be euphonic.

Padapoorvaardhavakrataa

Padapoorvaardhavakrataa relates to the use of padas in a sentence. In Sanskrit, a pada is a word to which a vibhakti has been added. Vibhakti is the marker which indicates the grammatical function of a pada in a sentence. Every pada has two parts: the first part is called padapurvaardh (the base word) and the terminal part or the suffix is known as padottaraardh (the vibhakti). Kuntak has considered the vakrataa in these two parts separately.

In Sanskrit when we use a noun in a sentence, we add a suffix (vibhakti) to it which indicates its number, gender and case. We can understand this with the help of an example. 'Krishna' is a noun, but we cannot use it in a sentence in Sanskrit unless we add the right vibhakti to it. If, for example, we add a visarga [(:) pronounced as aspirated 'ah'] to Krishna, it becomes 'Krishnah', that is, Krishna +

visarga (:). 'Krishnah' is a pada which can be used in a sentence. If we use 'Krishnah' in a sentence, this pada will indicate that it is a noun in the masculine gender, singular number and nominative case. So, the pada 'Krishnah' can be divided into two parts: prakriti and pratyay. 'Krishna' is the prakriti (or the base word) and the visarga (:) is the pratyay. The prakriti part of the pada 'Krishnah' is the padapuoovaardh and the pratyay part of it is the padottaraardh (terminal part). When a poet selects padas in such a way that their base parts (the first half) contribute to the charm of their lines, they are employing padapoorvaardhavakrataa.

Padottaraardhavakrataa

As we have seen, the literal meaning of padottaraardh is the terminal part of a pada. When a poet manipulates this part of the pada in order to achieve a particular effect, they are using padottaraardhavakrataa. This kind of vakrataa includes variations in the use of suffixes indicating tense, case, number, person, voice and particles. For example, the vakrataa of tense means that to describe something the poet might chooses a particular tense, and not some other, because they feel that by doing so they will make the writing more striking.

Vaakyavakrataa

Vaakyavakrataa means arranging the padas in a sentence (vaakya) in a particular manner. It is sometimes called vastuvakrataa. Kuntak says that for a skilled poet there are limitless possibilities of arranging padas in a sentence, but those possibilities depend on their skill and the effort they make.

To understand the concept of vaakyavakrataa, we should know how Sanskrit is different from other modern languages. Sanskrit is a fusional or inflected language—a type of synthetic language in which inflectional morphemes added to words decide the grammatical, syntactic or semantic function of a word. In other words, such languages use inflections (or addition of morpheme to the root word) to express the interrelationship between words in a sentence. Because of this grammatical property, words can be placed anywhere in a sentence and the sentence will still mean the same. This does not happen in analytical languages such as modern English or Hindi in which the position of a word in a sentence determines its grammatical function. For example, in the sentence 'Mohan played cricket' we cannot replace Mohan with 'cricket'. If we say 'Cricket played Mohan' we have changed the meaning of the sentence. This does not happen in a synthetic language like Sanskrit. For example, the sentence 'satyameva jayate' ('truth alone triumphs') can be written as 'jayate satyameva' and still it will mean the same. Because of this quality of the Sanskrit language, it is possible to arrange padas in a sentence in any order. That is the reason why this kind of vakrataa is possible in Sanskrit, but not in languages like modern English or Hindi.

Prakaraṇvakrataa

A prakaraṇ is an episode in a long narrative. Prakaraṇvakrataa means arranging sections, or parts of a poetic composition, in a certain order. It also means deciding which episodes in the narrative have to be highlighted. For example, if a number of incidents have to be described in a long story, the poet may decide to arrange them in a particular order so that the work becomes more appealing to the reader. The poet can also decide to narrate a particular episode in greater detail. Kuntak says that prakaraṇvakrataa also refers to the poet's ability to describe something in a convincing and lively manner.

Kuntak mentions different kinds of prakaraṇvakrataa. The first kind of prakaraṇvakrataa is, of course, the plotting of episodes in a particular order. Secondly, while narrating a story the writer may decide to pause for some time and describe some beautiful aspect of nature. For example, in the course of telling the story the writer may decide to describe a scene where the sun is rising, or is setting, or a beautiful garden or a lovely city, and so on. Thirdly, to make the story emotionally moving, the writer can describe how two characters meet unexpectedly. Fourthly, when telling a tale from history or mythology the writer can invent some details or incidents and make them part of their narrative. Again, Kuntak says that a playwright may decide to include a garbhaaNk (a play within a play) to make their play more interesting. We can say that by presenting a play within *Hamlet,* Shakespeare has practised prakaraṇvakrataa.

PrabaNdhavakrataa

PrabaNdh means a long literary work such as an epic, a long narrative poem or a play. Kuntak says that within reasonable limits a skilled poet can modify the established rules for writing a prabaNdh. When they do so, it is another kind of vakrataa called prabaNdhavakrataa. This kind of vakrataa can be of different types.

First, if the poet is telling a well known story in which a particular rasa predominates, they may decide to narrate the story in such a manner that some other rasa becomes prominent. In other words, the poet may decide to tell their story in such a way that the emotional impact on the reader is different from what the original story has.

Secondly, when narrating a well known story the writer may decide to end it abruptly at a point before it normally ends. For example, while narrating the story of the Ramayana if the writer concludes his story after the battle between Rama and Ravana and does not say anything about his journey to Ayodhya, the poet has used prabaNdhavakrataa. The only condition for doing so is that the poet should do it in such a manner that the primary rasa of the story is not diluted.

Thirdly, to make their story more interesting, the poet is free to introduce one or more subplots into it.

Fourthly, if the poet is narrating a well known story which has a famous title, they may decide to change the title. This too is a kind of prabaNdhavakrataa. For example, while retelling the Ramkathaa in which Urmila, Lakshman's wife, is the central character in Hindi, Maithilisharan Gupt chose to call his epic *Saaket* and not Ramkathaa or Ramayana. This is an example of prabaNdhavakrataa. The prabaNdhavakrataa of each poet is unique. For example, the story of the Ramayana as told by Valmiki was retold by many other writers, but each story looks different because the prabaNdhavakrataa of each poet is different.

Kuntak's great contribution to Sanskrit literary theory is that by conceptualising prakaraṇvakrataa and prabaNdhavakrataa he created two new methodologies for analysing and interpreting poetry.

Table 9.1: Types of Vakrokti

Kind of vakrokti	Meaning
varṇavinyaasavakrataa	a systematic arrangement of phonemes in verse
padapoorvaardhavakrataa	manipulation of the first half or the base part of a pada
padottaraardhavakrataa	variations in the use of suffixes indicating tense, case, number, person, voice and particles
vaakyavakrataa	arranging padas in a sentence in a particular order
prakaraṇvakrataa	manipulating sections or parts of a poetic composition
prabaNdhavakrataa	the skill of the poet displayed in handling different genres of prabaNdhkaavya such as an epic, a long narrative poem or a play

10

Auchitya

- ❖ The concept of auchitya
- ❖ Types of auchitya

THE CONCEPT OF AUCHITYA

The abstract noun auchitya has been derived from the adjective 'uchit' which means necessary or proper. Kshemendra in his *Auchityavicharcharcha* says,

> औचित्यं रससिद्धस्य स्थिरं काव्यस्य जीवितम्। (*औचित्यविचारचर्चा*)
>
> auchityaM rasasiddhasya sthiraM kaavyasya jeevitam |
> (*Auchityavicharcharcha*)
>
> Auchitya is the life breath of poetry which has rasa.

Then what is uchit or proper in literature? What is the context in which Kshemendra has used this word? He is using the word 'uchit' in the context of excellence in literary writing and by 'uchit' he means 'harmony'. When different elements in a literary composition or kaavya are used in such a manner that they are in harmony with one another and together create the effect the author wishes to create, we can say that the poem has the quality of auchitya.

We can understand the concept of auchitya with the help of an example. Let us imagine that we are watching a play. The play has a good plot, good stage presentation and so on, but there is a problem with the dialogue. The characters do not speak in the style that goes with their rank in society or with their educational background. For example, the king in a play speaks in a style which reminds the audience of a crude and uneducated braggart. That is wrong because a king should speak like a king. Since there is no harmony between the character's station in life and the language he uses in his speech, we would say that the play lacks auchitya in dialogue and to that extent fails as good art.

We can take another example of the need for auchitya in good literature. We have seen that good poetry is capable of generating rasa in the reader. If a poet's intention is to generate a particular rasa, for example the shriNgaar rasa, they might fail to do so because they use those consonant sounds which are not permitted in a poem of shriNgaar rasa. Here, the poem will fail as good art because the element of auchitya is missing in it. To evoke a particular rasa the poet must ensure that in the verse guṇas, alaNkaars and reeti are in harmony with one another.

Although Kshemendra—a scholar of the eleventh century—propounded the theory of auchitya, the concept predated him. Before him scholars were mainly concerned with elements like guṇas, rasa and alaNkaar, but the principle of auchitya was never considered worthy of independent study. However, they were familiar with the concept of auchitya.

Bharat is the first scholar to mention this concept but instead of the term auchitya he uses its synonym, anuroop. According to Bharat, drama is an imitation of life and therefore it is based on human behaviour (loka). That is why to decide whether something has been truly depicted in drama or not, one has to take human nature and social behaviour as the ultimate yardstick of literary realism. He writes,

> लोकसिद्धं भवेत् सिद्धं नाट्यं लोकस्वभावजम्,
> तस्मान्नाट्यप्रयोगे तु प्रमाणं लोक इष्यते। (*नाट्यशास्त्र*)
>
> loksiddhaM bhavet siddhaM natyaM lokaswabhaavajam,
> tasmaannaatyaprayoge tu pramaaṇaM loka iShyate ।
>
> (*Natyashastra*)
>
> Drama is an imitation of human behaviour in the world. Drama is born out of the behaviour and nature of human beings, therefore, (the authentic depiction of) human behaviour is the ultimate measure of truth in drama.

Bharat discusses the need for anuroop, that is, harmony and balance in drama. The purpose of acting is to evoke rasa or emotion in the audience. The combined effect of acting, text, alaNkaar, meter, music, voice, and all other elements of a play is that it results in rasa. For this to happen, the principle of anuroop must be followed at all times. He says that according to the principle of anuroop, the costume of the actor should go with his age; his movements should go with his costume; the text should go with the movements; and the acting should go with the text. If there is an absence of coordination between any of these things, there will be an absence of auchitya.

About auchitya, Bhamah says that a poet should keep in mind the fact that there is a correlation between what he writes and what really happens in the world. It is the real world that decides whether or not there is auchitya in poetry. According to him, used in the proper place, even flaws may become guṇas.

Dandin also considers auchitya an important element in poetry. If poetry contradicts the truth of place, time, art and social reality it will be seen as a flaw because such poetry lacks auchitya. Similarly, Vaman also has underlined the importance of auchitya in poetry. While discussing alaNkaars in his *Kavyalankar*, Rudrat also says that in the use of alaNkaars the principle of auchitya must be followed.

Kuntak also mentions auchitya in his *Vakroktijeevit* and says that it is a feature of vakrokti. Abhinavagupt (Kshemendra's teacher) however, is not prepared to place auchitya higher than rasa and dhwani. He believes that rasa and dhwani are fairly comprehensive principles which cover the element of auchitya also. According to him the fundamental element of auchitya is rasa. If a poem generates rasa, it will naturally possess the element of auchitya. He says that alaNkaar, guṇa and auchitya are supporters of rasa, which is the only defining feature of poetry. He feels that if a poet tries to create and achieve auchitya in his poetry without paying attention to rasa, the poet will be acting like a person who waters the leaves of a plant without watering its roots. Therefore, he does not think that it is necessary to treat auchitya as an independent literary principle. Mahim Bhatt, Abhinavagupt's teacher, also thinks that auchitya is nothing but the presence of rasa and where rasa is absent it is anauchitya, or the absence of auchitya.

Anandavardhan discusses auchitya in the third chapter of his *Dhwanyalok* at some length. He considers it to be necessary for the formation of rasa and asserts that the absence of auchitya is the only reason for rasabhaNg or the disruption of rasa. He writes,

> अनौचित्याद् ऋते नान्यद् रसभंगस्य कारणम्। (*ध्वन्यालोक*)
>
> anauchityaad rite naanyad rasabhaNgasya kaaraṇam। (*Dhwanyalok*)
>
> There is no other cause of the disruption of rasa than the absence of auchitya.

Kshemendra, however, believes that the presence of auchitya in a work of art is the fundamental cause of poetic excellence. One of the most reputed scholars of his time, Kshemendra is credited with writing over thirty books which include three important texts on poetics. He wrote drama, poetry and prose. His books on poetics are *Kavikanthabharan*, *Suvrittatilak* and *Auchityavicharcharcha*. The subject of *Kavikanthabharan* is poetry and the topics discussed include qualities and flaws of poetry and the training of a poet. *Suvrittatilak* is a work on prosody.

It is in *Auchityavicharcharcha* that Kshemendra's theory of auchitya is discussed in detail. He agrees with his teacher Abhinavagupt that rasa is important in poetry, but he also believes that what gives life to rasa is auchitya. In other words, in the absence of auchitya no poem can be beautiful. He goes on to say that auchitya is the cause of rasa and it is auchitya which causes a sense of wonder and miracle (chamatkaar) in a poem. He does accept the importance of guṇas and alaNkaars in poetry but places auchitya higher than these two elements. He goes on to say that in the absence of auchitya, 'guṇas are merely guṇas and alaNkaars are merely alaNkaars' but it is auchitya which 'can evoke rasa in poetry and is its very life'.

When Kshemendra calls auchitya 'the life of rasa' his premise is that the ultimate aim of poetry is to generate rasa in the sahridaya. Now, there are different elements which contribute to the generation of rasa. Among such elements, guṇas and alaNkaars have always been given the greatest importance. By placing auchitya higher than either guṇas or alaNkaars, Kshemendra introduces a new element into the discourse. He believes that in themselves guṇas or alaNkaars are not enough to generate rasa. In the absence of harmony, balance and consistency in the use of various literary devices, poetry cannot perform its primary function which is to generate rasa. Thus, he suggests that the principle of the interrelatedness of parts in poetry is of primary importance, in the absence of which it cannot achieve its potential of evoking feelings in the reader and giving them joy.

Kshemendra explains the principle of auchitya with the help of an example. He says that if a woman wears beautiful ornaments but on the wrong parts of her body, instead of looking beautiful she will look ridiculous. He further says that if a woman wears a waistband round her neck, a necklace on her waist, anklets on her arms and armbands around her ankles, who will not laugh at her? In the same manner, if a person is aggressive to a person who has come to them for protection, or shows compassion to their enemy, they will be laughed at because their conduct violates the principle of auchitya. In the same manner, while writing poetry a poet must always follow the principle of auchitya in order to be able to write good poetry. It is not enough for them to be able to use various kinds of styles and different poetic devices; the poet should also know when and in what measure should these devices be used. This understanding of harmony and consistency in art is what the principle of auchitya requires.

TYPES OF AUCHITYA

According to Kshemendra auchitya can be of countless types, but he identifies twenty-seven kinds which he considers the main varieties. These types can be classified into six broad categories which are related to (1) expression and form; (2) elements of poetry; (3) grammar; (4) authenticity or verisimilitude; (5) composition; (6) characterisation.

Auchitya Related to Expression and Form

The first kind of auchitya is related to the use of padas in a sentence. We have seen that a pada is a word to which the marker of its grammatical function has been added. In Sanskrit, only padas can be used in a sentence. A poet should choose padas with care and use them in such a manner that the beauty of the lines is enhanced. To illustrate his point, Kshemendra says that as a dark-coloured tilak (an ornamental mark) placed on the forehead of a fair-skinned woman and a light-coloured tilak on a dark-skinned woman help enhance their beauty, the right pada at the right place adds to the beauty of the entire line in poetry.

Another kind of auchitya is that which is seen in the use of vaakya (sentences). When writing sentences, a poet should ensure that the reader is able not only to understand them easily but also to experience the right rasa. For example, if a poet compares the arms of Duryodhan (the great Kaurava warrior in the Mahabharata) to lotus stems their sentence will lack auchitya because this comparison is used when describing the delicate arms of a woman.

The third kind of auchitya related to form and expression is that which must be ensured in a prabaNdh or a literary composition. While writing in a particular genre, a poet should make sure that all the sentences in the composition are properly related to one another and that together they help in conveying the poet's intended sense.

Auchitya Related to Elements of Poetry

There are three kinds of auchitya which are related to the use of the various elements of poetry. These types are concerned with guṇ as, alaNkaars and rasa. When writing a poem, a poet should make sure that their language expresses the right guṇa. For example, if a great warrior like Ashwatthama describes the battlefield as an ocean of war full of tumult and churning with violence and its sound is like that of the crack of thunder in the clouds which fills the earth and the sky with an uproar never heard before, his language expresses the right guṇa (that is, the oja guṇa) because these words have been spoken by a man of incomparable heroism and courage. But if the same kind of language is used by a person with a totally different character (a lover, for example), it will lack auchitya because such a character would never speak in the language of Ashwatthama.

The next kind of auchitya relates to the use of alaNkaars. It means that a poet should use the right kind of alaNkaar to embellish their description. For instance, in his play *Ratnavali*, Emperor Harsha (606–648CE) describes the visit of King Udayan, the king of Vatsa and also the hero of his play, to the Spring Festival. Harsha compares the coming of Udayan to the appearance of the God of Love (Kamadev) himself. Here Harsha has used the upamaa alaNkaar (a simile) and has followed the principle of auchitya in the use of this alaNkaar. There is auchitya in the use of this alaNkaar because there are several similarities between Udayan and Kamadev. Since Udayan has conquered all, he has no need to fight anyone anymore. Similarly, since Kamadev does not possess a body, he cannot fight anyone physically. Another similarity between King Udayan and Kamadev is that if the king has rati (the feeling of conjugal love) in his heart, Kamadev also has Rati, who is his wife and the Hindu goddess of love representing carnal desire. Thirdly, King Udayan is loved by everyone and lives in everyone's heart because he is a good and kind ruler. Kamadev also lives as love in everyone's heart and is loved by all. And finally, as King Udayan likes his friend and jester Vasantak (the name means spring), Kamadev also likes vasant (the spring season) which is the season of beauty and growth.

Finally, while writing their poem, the poet should pay attention to the rasa they intend to generate. There should be a correlation between form and style and the emotional impact the poet's work has on the reader. Kshemendra says that as the Ashoka tree in spring pleases everyone, in the same manner because of the justness of rasa, a particular emotion grows in everyone's heart and pleases them.

Auchitya Related to Grammar

Kshemendra mentions seven kinds of auchitya which are concerned with the correct use of language. He mentions the correct use of verb, case, gender, number, adjective, prefix and particles. If a poet uses grammatically correct language, they will be able to achieve auchitya in the use of language. Here he includes even the use of particles, which are words or parts of words which have a grammatical function but have often little or no meaning. For an illustration of the right use of particles, we can take an example from Kshemendra's own book *Munimatmimansa* where the author criticises all those men who perform hundreds of yajnas pouring a great deal of ghee (clarified butter) into fire pits so that they can earn puṇya (benefit of good deeds) and to go to heaven. When they die, they indeed go to heaven where they spend a short time till all their puṇya is exhausted. After that, they are driven out of heaven in the same manner as lustful and sensual men who have lost their wealth are thrown out by prostitutes. Kshemendra says that such puṇya is short lived and wise men do not run after it. Then he addresses people who wish to earn puṇya by performing rituals and says, 'O fools! Therefore, instead of that kind of puṇya, you should wish for the joy of contemplation and contentment which are the only things that are true and eternal (satyaM cha nityaM cha)'. Here 'cha' ('and') is a particle which has been repeated, although grammatically it was not necessary to do it. By repeating this particle Kshemendra has achieved balance in the rhythm of the line making it more pleasing to the ear. This is an example of auchitya in the use of a particle.

Auchitya Related to Authenticity

Kshemendra says that in handling material for a composition a poet should try to adhere to the principle of auchitya. This auchitya can be of five different kinds: the auchitya of kaal (time), desh (region or the location of the action), kul (the clan to which the hero belongs), vrat (a vow that a character has taken) and tattva (a true and objective description of the character and action). The auchitya of kaal (time) requires that while describing something the time when it happened must be kept in mind. For example, a description of the spring season while expressing the shriNgaar rasa will be an uchit (proper) description of the background because such a description would enhance the rasa. Describing some other season not suited to the rasa would mean an absence of the auchitya of kaal or time.

In the same manner, a poet should ensure that their description of a location or region (desh) is true and faithful. For an example of the auchitya of the clan (kulauchitya) we can refer to the Ramayana. The hero of the Ramayana is Rama. He belongs to the Ikshwaaku clan, which is famous for its high moral standards and commitment to duty. When Valmiki describes Rama, he keeps in the mind the glorious tradition of the Ikshwaku clan and describes his hero accordingly. Therefore, Valmiki achieves the auchitya of clan in his poetry which makes his description of the hero more convincing. The auchitya of vrat refers to the vows that an ascetic takes when they renounce the world. The poem should describe it truly. Finally, there is the auchitya of tattva which convinces the reader that what they are reading has been truthfully described.

Auchitya Related to Composition

Elements related to the composition of a literary text should be used properly. The auchitya of sattva (vigour or inner strength) is related to characterisation. The author should delineate a character in a proper manner so that their essential qualities are conveyed. The auchitya of abhipraay (intention) and swabhaav are also related to characterisation and are concerned with the justness of the use of dialogue and description. The author should be able to express the intention of the character and also their basic nature. Summarising (saarsaNgrah) anything properly is also a kind of auchitya in composition. The auchitya of pratibhaa mentioned by Kshemendra is concerned with a display of creativity in writing.

Auchitya Related to Characterisation

The poet should keep in mind the principle of auchitya while describing the age (avasthaa) of a character. The auchitya of vichaar is the expression of proper thoughts. The auchitya related to name (naam) enjoins upon the poet to choose the names of his characters carefully so that they reflect the personality of the character. Finally, the poet should also be careful about how they incorporate words used for blessing someone (aasheervachan) in theirpoem.

Table 10.1: Types of Auchitya

Category	Type of Auchitya
Expression and form	1. pada (word with its grammatical marker) 2. vaakya (sentences) 3. prabaNdha (literary composition, mainly poetry)
Elements of poetry	1. guṇa 2. alaNkaar 3. rasa
Grammar	1. verb and verbal construct 2. case and declensions 3. gender 4. number 5. adjectives 6. prefix 7. particles
Authenticity	1. kaal (time) 2. desh (region) 3. kul (clan) 4. vrat (vow) 5. tattva (objectivity)
Composition	1. sattva, or inner strength and vigour 2. abhipraay, or purpose 3. swabhaav, or nature 4. saarsaNgrah, or summary 5. pratibhaa, or imagination
Characterisation	1. avasthaa, or the age of a person 2. vichaar, or good thoughts 3. naam, that is characters should be named according to what they do 4. aasheervachan, or benediction

Auchitya is not an element of poetry. It is rather a condition which must be fulfilled if a poem has to succeed in its ultimate objective of generating the right rasa in the reader. The principle of auchitya requires that alaNkaars, guṇas, description, dialogue, characterisation and all other elements of creative writing must be judiciously employed by the poet. Auchitya is actually related to poetic intelligence, which ensures that the poet is able to produce the literary text they want.

11

Flaws in Poetry

- Meaning of kaavya doSha
- Types of doShas

Meaning of Kaavya DoSha

In Indian poetics, whenever scholars have mentioned the guṇas of poetry, they have also spoken of its doShas or flaws. Obviously, both guṇas and doShas are relative terms and there are no absolute standards which can be set for either of them. The simplest definition of doSha is that it is the opposite of guṇa and whatever helps poetry achieve the poet's end is a guṇa and whatever militates against it is a doSha.

A doSha can relate both to the sound and sense of an expression. When the reader feels that something is missing or has been done wrongly, there is a doSha in the poem. Beginning with Bharat, scholars have tried to identify, name and classify the various kinds of flaws in poetry.

Bharat's *Natyashastra* is the first text in which we find a description of flaws in poetry, or in drama, to be more specific. Here he does not really define the term 'doSha' but merely says that all those elements that neutralise the guṇas are flaws in poetry. In Chapter 17 of the *Natyashastra* he mentions ten such flaws that weaken the effect of drama. Among such defects, he includes using a wrong synonym for a word; trying to describe what is beyond description; writing words in a poem that do not convey any sense; using a word in a sense that is different from its commonly understood meaning; ignoring the different connotations of a word; not expressing one's meaning clearly; making a statement without proof; using words without saNdhi, that is, without the proper joining of vowel sounds;

using a defective meter; and using non-words in poetry. Despite mentioning these flaws, Bharat, unlike his successors, displays a somewhat tolerant attitude towards writers who make these mistakes. He accepts that since nothing in this world is flawless, scholars should not be too critical of writers in whose writing some of these flaws are seen.

Among the successors of Bharat, Bhamah is one of those scholars who has discussed the flaws of poetry in considerable detail. In his *Kavyalankar* there are about a hundred and seventy verses that deal with flaws in poetry. The entire fifth chapter of the book is concerned with the treatment of kaavya doShas. When it comes to the presence of doShas in poetry, Bhamah is extremely rigid and unforgiving. He says that a poet should not allow even a single flaw in their poetry and a doSha in poetry should be condemned like a bad son. He goes to the extent of saying that a good poet never leaves any scope for flaws in their poetry.

Dandin, who came after Bhamah is also not ready to tolerate even a small flaw in poetry. He says that a poem fails because of kaavya doShas and adds that poets and scholars should avoid these flaws. Like Bharat, he also mentions ten doShas many of which are the same as those Bharat lists. Dandin thinks that to be successful a poet should have the ability to identify the guṇas and doShas in their poetry.

Like Dandin, Vaman also sees doShas as the opposite of guṇas. In his *Kavyalankarsutra* he says that elements that destroy the beauty of poetry are known as kaavya doShas. It is a very comprehensive definition of doShas and includes all kinds of mistakes that a poet might make while writing a poem. He identifies two kinds of doShas: those related to the wrong use of language and those displaying the poet's inability to convey their intended meaning. In his *Kavyalankarsutra* he mentions also twenty doShas of poetry which relate to errors in the use of vocabulary as well as of syntax. Almost following Vaman, Rudrat mentions twenty-three doShas which include flaws related to the wrong use of vocabulary, syntax, faulty use of similes and the inability to convey the intended meaning.

Anandavardhan discusses flaws related to rasa and calls them rasa doSha. Anything that works as a barrier to the generation of rasa is rasa doSha. He says that there are some doShas which are to be flaws in all conditions. For example, ungrammatical language (chyutsaNskriti) will always be seen as a fault, but there are some doShas which become positive qualities in some specific conditions. Those doShas which are barriers to the expression of a rasa may not always be flaws in all conditions. For example, shrutikaTu (using harsh sounding words) is a doSha in the expression of shriNgaar rasa but the same flaw becomes a positive quality when a rasa like raudra is being expressed.

Mahim Bhatt, the eleventh century Kashmiri scholar, discusses the various flaws in poetry in his *Vyaktivivek*. According to him anauchitya or absence of auchitya (that is, lack of functional balance and proportion in a literary text) is the primary flaw in poetry. According to him, the primary kind of anauchitya is the absence of rasa. In simple terms it means that a poem which fails to evoke any emotion in the reader is flawed because the primary function of poetry is to generate emotion in the sahridaya, and by doing so, give joy to them. He has classified this kind of flaw into two categories: antaraNg (internal) and bahiraNg (external). The first kind relates to flaws that directly affect the expression of rasa, while the second type includes all the other flaws. He believes that such doShas creep into poetry mainly because the poet is careless.

In the seventh ullaas (chapter) of his *Kavyaprakash*, Mammat discusses different kinds of flaws in poetry. He begins the chapter by defining what a flaw is:

मुख्यार्थहतिर्दोषो रसश्च मुख्यस्तदाश्रयाद्वाच्यः,
उभयोपयोगिनः स्युः शब्दाद्यास्तेन तेष्वपि सः। (*काव्यप्रकाश*)

mukhyaarthahatirdoSho rasashcha mukhyastadaashrayaadvaachyah,
ubhayopayoginah syuh shabdaadyaastena teShwapi sah ।
(*Kavyaprakash*)

That which weakens the primary meaning is a flaw. And in poetry the rasa (emotions, sentiment, et cetera) constitutes the primary meaning. The literal meaning of a poem (vaachyaarth) is supported by the rasa

> in it, and therefore that meaning is also a part of the primary meaning. Both rasa and meaning are supported by words (the language of poetry) and therefore a flaw in language is also a flaw in poetry.

What Mammat is saying is that rasa is the primary meaning of a poem. In other words, the primary function of a poem is to evoke emotion in the reader. Now, rasa is generated by the right use of words in both their denotative and connotative senses. Any fault in the use of language will ultimately act as a barrier to the generation of rasa. When this happens, the poem will fail to achieve its fundamental objective. Thus, using flawless language is of prime importance in poetry. Mammat identifies three kinds of flaws in poetry: (1) those that relate to rasa niShpatti (that is, the generation of rasa); (2) those that act as barriers to the expression of meaning; and (3) those that involve a faulty use of words. These three kinds of flaws are interrelated.

TYPES OF DOSHAS OR FLAWS IN POETRY

Taking into account the various kinds of flaws in poetry discussed by different scholars from the time of Bharat onwards, we can now classify the major kaavya doShas into three broad categories:

- pada doSha (flaws related to the use of vocabulary)
- artha doSha (inability to convey the intended meaning)
- rasa doSha (barriers to the creation of rasa)

Flaws Related to the Use of Vocabulary (Pada DoSha)

There are a number of flaws in the use of vocabulary. Many of these errors relate to the use of sentences also. Some of the major flaws are given below.

ShrutikaTu

The term 'shrutikaTu' means 'harsh sounding'. When a poet uses words full of harsh consonant sounds it has the flaw of shrutikaTu. Bhamah uses the word 'shrutikaShTa' for it. It means that if a poet uses a word which disturbs the rhythm or music of the line it will be classified under this flaw. It also means that a poet is allowed to use words with various kinds of sounds to enhance the emotional appeal of the poem, but at no time can the poet afford to be unmusical or to use language that is aurally not pleasing.

ChyutsaNskriti

If a poet uses ungrammatical expressions, this is known as the flaw of chyutsaNskriti. A good poet is expected to use grammatically correct language. Vaman and Bhojdev have used the term 'asaadhu' for this kind of flaw and Bhamah and Dandin call this defect 'shabdaheen'. Our scholars do not allow a poet to take liberties with grammar in the name of poetic license.

Aprayuktatva

According to Rudrat, an expression that is grammatically correct and conveys a perfectly intelligible sense but is not used by poets in their works is a flaw called aprayuktatva. This flaw has also been called 'aprateet'. Bhojdev, Mammat and the *Agni Purana* mention this flaw. Classical Sanskrit poetics lays great stress on the right kind of poetic diction and therefore a marked deviation from the traditional way of writing is seen as a flaw.

KliShTataa

To ensure that the poem is easily understood by the reader, a poet should avoid using difficult (kliShTa) words in it. KliShTa words refer to those words that people do not normally use. It also includes those expressions which are so elliptical that a reader has to try very hard to make sense of it.

Anuchitaarth

A word may have a well-known meaning and a lesser known one. When a poet uses a word in its lesser-known sense it is seen as a doSha because it has been used in its anuchit (improper) sense. For example, if a poet uses the word 'shoṇit' to describe the redness of the heroine's lips, they may be guilty of having used a word in its anuchitaarth, or 'improper sense'. The word 'shoṇit' has two different meanings. Its commonly known meaning is 'blood' while its lesser-known meaning is 'redness'. When a reader finds that the poet has used 'shoṇit' to describe the heroine's lips the first image that comes to his mind is that of blood, which is not the intended sense of the poet. The poet's intention is to describe the red lusciousness of the heroine's lips. By using a word in its anuchit (improper) arth (meaning) the poet has committed a mistake and there is now the kaavya doSha of anuchitaarth in their poetry.

Ashleeltaa

'Ashleel' means an expression which is obscene or disgusting and which creates a feeling of embarrassment in the reader. If a poet uses a word that has this kind of effect on the reader, they are guilty of the kaavya doSha called ashleeltaa. According to Vaman, when a word has two meanings (one of which is obscene) and still a poet uses that word in their poem, they will be guilty of the flaw of ashleeltaa. According to our scholars, ashleeltaa is always undesirable in literature because it militates against its fundamental purpose, which is to promote sattva guṇa in the reader. Sattva guṇa is characterised by goodness of heart, purity of character and tranquility of mind.

Graamyatva

This flaw in poetry is mentioned for the first time by Bharat. In the *Natyashastra*, graamyatva has been called 'bhinnaarth'. According to him, when a word expresses some crude or vulgar meaning it is called graamyatva. According to the principles of classical literature, a poet should not use language which uncultured people employ in their day-to-day conversation. If there is such an expression in their poetry it will be said to have the flaw of graamyatva.

Asamartha

The literal meaning of asamartha is 'incapable'. When a pada is unable to convey its intended meaning, it is known as the fault of asamartha. Vaman was the first to mention this fault in poetry. Explaining the idea further, Bhojdev says that when padas which logically do not go with one another are used together, one or more of them may lose their ability to convey their intended sense and then it will be seen as a fault called asamartha doSha.

Nirarthak

Words which a poet uses only to complete the meter and which do not add anything to the meaning are called nirarthak words. Vaman has used the term 'anarthak' for such words. For example, Rudrat says that if a poet uses an adjective just for the sake of completing the meter and not for qualifying a noun, they will be guilty of nirarthak doSha. For example, if someone writes 'He was a brave hero' or 'It is a true fact', it is a fault because 'hero' and 'fact' contain the meaning of 'brave' and 'true' respectively. Similarly, Mammat says that many poets use 'cha' (which means 'and') repeatedly to complete the meter. This is a flaw in their poetry.

Pratikoolvarṇataa

The use of certain consonant sounds is prohibited while expressing a particular rasa. While depicting a rasa if a poet uses consonant sounds which are not permitted in that rasa, they would be guilty of pratikoolvarṇataa. For example, in shriNgaar rasa, all the five consonants of the /t/ group in the Devanagari script (such as the hard /t/, hard /th/, hard /d/, hard /dh/, et cetera) are prohibited. If a poet uses words like 'madhurkanTha' (sweet voice), 'utkanTha' (eagerness), and so on, in a poem depicting love they would be guilty of pratikoolvarṇataa.

Table 11.1: Flaws Related to the Use of Vocabulary (Pada DoSha)

Flaw	**Meaning**
shrutikaTu	using unpleasant sounding words
chyutsaNskriti	using ungrammatical expressions
aprayuktatva	using words not commonly used in poetry
kliShTataa	using words that are difficult to understand
anuchitaarth	using a word in its lesser-known sense
ashleeltaa	using obscene expressions
graamyatva	using expressions which uncultured people use

(Contd.)

Table 11.1: (*Contd.*)

Flaw	Meaning
asamartha	the inability of a pada to convey its intended meaning
nirarthak	using words just to complete the meter
pratikoolvarṇataa	using words with those consonant sounds which are not permitted in a rasa

Inability to Convey the Intended Meaning (Artha DoSha)

When a poet is unable to express their intended meaning, it is seen as a flaw. Scholars have mentioned a large number of such weaknesses in expression. Most of these flaws can be classified under such categories as lack of lucidity; absence of conciseness; not paying attention to the consistency of ideas; overlooking the question of the propriety of an expression; and similar other flaws that go against the principles of successful literary communication. Some of the more prominent artha doShas are given below.

Punaruktatva

When the same idea is repeated without adding anything to the beauty of poetry, it is the fault of punaruktatva. Bharat has used the term 'ekaarth' for this flaw. According to Bharat, when a number of words are used to convey the same meaning, it is the fault of ekaarth. The English term for this is tautology.

KaShTaarth

When it is difficult to understand the meaning of an expression it is seen as a fault and this flaw has been called kaShTaarth. If a poet uses a term that is used only in a particular subject, they would be guilty of making this mistake. For example, if a poet uses the word 'aashay' in place of 'saNskaar' it is flawed, because 'aashay' is used as a synonym for 'saNskaar' only in the *Yogashastra* and not elsewhere.

Akramatva

When things are mentioned in an order that goes against their natural sequence it is known as akramatva doSha. 'Akramatva' means 'not in sequence'. For instance, if someone uses the words 'sow', 'flower', 'sprout', and 'fruition' one after another, they are guilty of this fault because the word 'sprout' should have been used after 'sow' and before 'flower'.

Vyaahatatva

When one part of the expression contradicts another part, it is a fault known as vyaahatatva. This is a weakness in expression and confuses the reader which prevents them from enjoying the poem.

Vidyaaviruddha DoSha

According to Dandin, if a poet says something that goes against the customs of a place; spirit of the time; norms of arts, scriptures, justice, popular sentiments; and so on, it will be seen as a fault in their poetry. Vaman thinks that if a poet says something that goes against the principles of the arts and contradicts the shaastras, it is vidyaaviruddha doSha. Mammat says that any statement that contradicts the *Dharmashastras*, *Arthashastra*, *Kamashastra* and *Yogashastra* has vidyaaviruddha doSha.

Table 11.2: Inability to Convey the Intended Meaning (Artha DoSha)

Flaw	Meaning
punaruktatva	use of tautology
kaShTaarth	using words that are difficult to understand
akramatva	mentioning things in the wrong sequence
vyaahatatva	contradiction
vidyaaviruddha dosha	contradicting received wisdom

Flaws Related to Rasa (Rasa DoSha)

There may also be flaws in poetry which come in the way of the generation of rasa. Scholars like Bhamah, Dandin and Vaman limit themselves to the discussion of flaws in the use of language and weaknesses in communicating intended meaning, but there are others who have discussed those flaws which act as barriers to rasa. Although all kinds of flaws in poetry ultimately act as barriers to the creation of rasa, there are some which are specifically concerned with rasa.

The KaShTakalpanaa of Vibhaav and Anubhaav

When a poet describes something in such a manner that it is difficult to know the nature of the vibhaav, anubhaav, or both, it is seen as a flaw in poetry. Mammat gives an example of this flaw. He refers to a verse in which the poet writes, 'He is losing interest in things and he is losing his ability to decide what is real; he feels weakened and faints again and again. It is unfortunate that his body is going through such a difficult condition, now what can one do about this?' The poet is saying that someone is feeling restless and weak. We can only presume that this has happened because of a woman with whom the man referred to is in love. But this can happen to a person in some other rasa also such as karuṇ or vibhatsa. By not mentioning the cause of the man's behaviour the poet has made a mistake.

In the same manner, Mammat has also mentioned the kaShTakalpanaa in determining the anubhaav. Giving an example of the uncertainty about anubhaav, Mammat refers to a verse in which a poet describes how a young man sees a beautiful woman who is fair like the rising moon and how the manner in which she has covered her head with the end of her sari cannot conceal her rising breasts. Mammat says that the poet here is trying to evoke the shriNgaar rasa. He mentions the heroine who is the aalaMban vibhaav. He also mentions the rising moon, which is the uddeepan vibhaav, but he fails to describe the feelings of the hero on seeing the woman. Therefore, he fails to mention the anubhaavs which are caused in the hero when he sees the heroine. The reader has to make an effort to understand the reaction of the hero because the anubhaavs have not been described. This is a flaw related to the generation of rasa.

Swashabdavaachyataa

This kind of doSha means that the poet *names* an emotion but does not *evoke* it. When in their description a poet mentions a particular rasa or some bhaav such as the sthaayibhaav or the saNchaareebhaavs without actually evoking them, it will be a rasa doSha. For example, if a poet writes that when the hero saw that man in pain, 'karuṇ rasa was born in him', the poet is making the error of swashabdavaachyataa, or naming the rasa instead of evoking it.

AkaaṇD Prathan

This kind of rasa doSha means that the poet ignores the main rasa and introduces some other rasa. In other words, there should be consistency in the manner in which a rasa is evoked. Giving an example of this rasa doSha, Mammat says that in *Venisamhara*, when heroes like Bheeshma are dying, the poet describes a love scene between Duryodhana and Bhanumati. Here the introduction of shriNgaar rasa at a time when the context does not demand it is a flaw in poetry.

AnaNga Varṇan

When a poet highlights something that is not connected with the main rasa this is treated as a fault. Mammat gives an example from *Karpuramanjari*, Rajshekhar's play in Prakrit. In the play, the king praises the prisoner's description of the spring season while ignoring the same kind of description made by the heroine and even by himself. Here the poet has highlighted something related to a minor character while ignoring the main characters. This works against the evocation of the primary rasa and therefore the poet is guilty of the rasa doSha of anaNga varṇan.

Prakritiviparyay

When a poet describes those qualities in a hero which are not seen in that kind of character, they are making the error of prakritiviparyay. In classical Sanskrit drama and poetry, heroes have been classified into three kinds: (1) divya (celestial), that is, heroes such as gods; (2) adivya (non-celestial), that is, heroes such as kings and so on; and (3) divyaadivya (either celestial or non-celestial), heroes such as avataars (incarnations of gods as men) or a great man with exceptional abilities. These three classes of heroes have specific natural qualities. If a poet describes a hero in a manner which is different from the natural qualities of that class of heroes, it is a rasa doSha because it will come in the way of the creation of rasa. For example, a poet cannot depict shriNgaar rasa if the hero is a god or is someone who is regarded as a parent, such as in the character of Sita in the Ramayana. If the poet does that, it will be treated as a fault in their poetry. Prakritiviparyay also means describing something which contradicts the customs of a place, or time, or the natural traits of a character. In other words, the poet has to be credible at all times.

Table 11.3: Flaws Related to Rasa (Rasa DoSha)

Flaw	Meaning
kaShTakalpanaa of vibhaav and anubhaav	lack of clarity about vibhaav and anubhaav
swashabdavaachyataa	naming the emotion rather than evoking it
akaaṇD prathan	ignoring the main rasa and introducing some other rasa
anaNga varṇan	highlighting something not connected with the main rasa
prakritiviparyay	improper description of a hero and going against time, place and character

Glossary

aakaaNkShaa	आकांक्षा	fulfilling the expectation of complete melaning in a sentence
aakhyaayikaa	आख्यायिका	a story in Sanskrit in which the protagonist tells his/her own story and uses a mixture of prose and verse
aalaMban vibhaav	आलंबन विभाव	the thing or person that causes emotion in the aashray
aanaNd	आनंद	transcendental bliss
aasheervachan	आशीर्वचन	benediction
aashray	आश्रय	the person in whom the aalaMban vibhaav arouses emotion
aatmaa	आत्मा	soul
abhidhaa	अभिधा	literal meaning
abhidhaamoolaadhwani	अभिधामूलाध्वनि	suggested meaning derived from abhidhaa
abhipraay	अभिप्राय	purport
abhyaas	अभ्यास	practice
adbhut	अद्‌भुत	wonderful
adrishT	अदृष्ट	that which cannot be seen
akaaṇD prathan	अकाण्ड प्रथन	ignoring the main rasa
akramatva	अक्रमत्व	mentioning things in the wrong order
alaNkaar	अलंकार	a figure of speech
alaNkaardhwani	अलंकारध्वनि	suggested meaning of an expression based on the alaNkaars present
alaNkaarshaastra	अलंकारशास्त्र	the science or study of figures of speech; poetics
alaukik	अलौकिक	transcendental
anaNga varṇan	अनंग वर्णन	highlighting something not connected to the main rasa

anibaddha kaavya	अनिबद्ध काव्य	a work made up of a number of independent verses
anubhaav	अनुभाव	the consequent of vibhaav
anuchitaarth	अनुचितार्थ	using a word in it's lesser-known or more obscure sense
anupraas	अनुप्रास	alliteration
apahaasit	अपहासित	vulgar laughter
aprayuktattva	अप्रयुक्तत्व	an expression not used by poets in their works
artha	अर्थ	meaning; also gaining material wealth
artha doSha	अर्थ दोष	inability to convey the intended meaning
arthaalaNkaar	अर्थालंकार	a figure of speech that depends on the meaning of the expression and not on the words used in it
arthavyakti	अर्थव्यक्ति	clear expression of meaning
asamarth	असमर्थ	when an expression fails to convey its intended meaning; incapable
ashleeltaa	अश्लीलता	obscenity
atihaasit	अतिहासित	excessive laughter
atishayokti	अतिशयोक्ति	hyperbole
auchitya	औचित्य	the principle of harmony and consistency in literary writing
avasthaa	अवस्था	a person's age
baNdha	बंध	organisation of the verse
bhaaShya	भाष्य	explanation
bhaav	भाव	emotion
bhayaanak	भयानक	fear
bheda	भेद	type
brahmaanaNd sahodar	ब्रह्मानन्द सहोदर	equal to experiencing the divine
chamatkaar	चमत्कार	miracle; marvel
champoo	चंपू	a work which is a blend of prose and verse
chitra kaavya	चित्र काव्य	a poem in which the literal meaning completely overshadows its suggested meaning

chitraalaNkaar	चित्रालंकार	typographical arrangement of words in a poem to create a shape
chyutsaNskriti	च्युतसंस्कृति	ungrammatical
daanav	दानव	demon
daanaveer	दानवीर	a charitable hero/person
darshan	दर्शन	philosophy
deeptivistaar	दीप्तिविस्तार	a state of mind characterised by a feeling of being liberated or an expansion of awareness
dharm	धर्म	virtue
dharmaveer	धर्मवीर	a dutiful hero/person
dhwani	ध्वनि	suggested meaning
dhwani kaavya	ध्वनि काव्य	a poem in which the suggested meaning is the most prominent
doSha	दोष	defect
driShT	दृष्ट	that which can be seen
drishya kaavya	दृश्य काव्य	drama
druti	द्रुति	to flow or melt; a state of mind caused by maadhurya guṇa
garbhaaNk	गर्भांक	a play within a play
gauDee reeti	गौडी रीति	that reeti or diction which is primarily associated with oja guṇa; is ornate, baroque and is rolling in its movement
graamyatva	ग्राम्यत्व	use of crude, non-literary language in poetry
guṇa	गुण	quality
guṇibhootavyaNgya kaavya	गुणिभूतव्यंग्य काव्य	a poem in which the suggested meaning is secondary and the literal meaning is primary
haasit	हासित	smile
haasya	हास्य	mirth
hetu	हेतु	cause or reason
kaama	काम	desire
kaanti	कान्ति	that loveliness which is born out of novelty and freshness of expression

kaarikaa	कारिका	a short verse meant to be memorised
kaavya	काव्य	literature, poetry
kaavyahetu	काव्यहेतु	causes of poetic creation
kaavyalakShaṇ	काव्यलक्षण	features of poetry
kaavyaprayojan	काव्यप्रयोजन	purpose of poetry
kaavyashaastra	काव्यशास्त्र	poetics
kaayik	कायिक	related to the body
kalaashrit	कलाश्रित	a work based on some art
kalpit	कल्पित	a story that is entirely imaginary
karuṇ	करुण	sorrow
kaShTaarth	कष्टार्थ	an expression that is difficult to understand
kaShTakalpanaa	कष्टकल्पना	difficult to know
kathaa	कथा	a story in prose which can be written in Sanskrit, Prakrit or Apabhramsha
kavi	कवि	poet
keerti	कीर्ति	fame
khyaatavritt	ख्यातवृत्त	a work based on a well known story
kliShTataa	क्लिष्टता	unintelligibility
kriyaakalp	क्रियाकल्प	another term for kaavyashastra, or the theory and practice of poetry
krodh	क्रोध	anger
laakShaṇik	लाक्षणिक	same as lakShak
lakShak	लक्षक	a word that has an indicated meaning
lakShaṇaa	लक्षणा	indicated meaning
lakShaṇaamoolaadhwani	लक्षणामूलाध्वनि	suggested meaning based on the lakShaṇaa
lakShyaarth	लक्ष्यार्थ	the indicated meaning of a word
maadhurya	माधुर्य	sweetness (one of the guṇas of poetry)
mahaakaavya	महाकाव्य	epic
mokSh	मोक्ष	salvation

mukhyaarth	मुख्यार्थ	literal meaning
naam	नाम	name
naaTak	नाटक	drama
naTya	नाट्य	dance or drama
neeras	नीरस	without rasa
nibaddha kaavya	निबद्ध काव्य	a work which has a well-defined structure
nihitaartha	निहितार्थ	using a word in its lesser-known sense
nipuṇataa	निपुणता	expertise
nirarthak	निरर्थक	unnecessary words used just to complete the meter
oja	ओज	one of the guṇas of poetry characterised by energy and power
paak	पाक	maturity
pada	पद	a word to which the marker of its grammatical function has been added according to the rules of Sanskrit grammar
pada doSh	पद दोष	flaws related to the use of vocabulary
padapurvaardhavakrataa	पदपूर्वार्धवक्रता	arranging padas according to their substantive parts
padottaraardhavakrataa	पदोत्तरार्धवक्रता	arranging padas according to their terminal parts
paNchaalee reeti	पांचाली रीति	that reeti or diction that is primarily associated with prasaad guṇa; style and diction falls midway between gauDee and vaidarbhee reetis
prabaNdha	प्रबंध	literary composition, mainly poetry
prabaNdhavakrataa	प्रबंधवक्रता	organising matter in a poem
prakaraṇvakrataa	प्रकरणवक्रता	organising sections of a long poem
prakriti	प्रकृति	the substantive part of a pada
prakritiviparyay	प्रकृतिविपर्यय	attributing wrong qualities to the hero

prasaad	प्रसाद	one of the guṇas of poetry characterised by the quality of lucidity
prateeyamaan artha	प्रतीयमान अर्थ	suggested meaning
pratibhaa	प्रतिभा	natural talent
pratikoolvarṇataa	प्रतिकूलवर्णता	using those consonant sounds which are not allowed while expressing a rasa
pratyay	प्रत्यय	suffix
prayojan	प्रयोजन	purpose
preeti	प्रीति	the delight experienced by the audience while reading or writing poetry
punaruktatva	पुनरुक्तत्व	the flaw of tautology
punarukti	पुनरुक्ति	repetition
puṇya	पुण्य	benefits of good deeds according to Hinduism
raakShas	राक्षस	demon
raamkathaa	रामकथा	the story of Rama
raja	रज	a state of consciousness higher than tama and lower than sattva, characterised by passion and activity
rasa doSha	रस दोष	obstruction in the generation of rasa
rasa	रस	aesthetically experienced emotion
rasa niShpatti	रस निष्पत्ति	the generation of rasa
rasabhaNga	रसभंग	disruption of the rasa
rasadhwani	रसध्वनि	suggested meaning of an expression capable of evoking rasa or emotion
rati	रति	erotic love
raudra	रौद्र	anger
reeti	रीति	diction
roopak	रूपक	as an alaNkaar it means metaphor; it also means a play
saadhaaraṇeekaraṇ	साधारणीकरण	generalisation of emotion

saahitya	साहित्य	literature
saahityashaastra	साहित्यशास्त्र	the discipline of literature
saarsaNgraha	सारसंग्रह	summary
saatvik bhaav	सात्विक भाव	involuntary action
sahajaalaNkaar	सहजालंकार	natural grace
sahridaya	सहृदय	a cultivated reader
samaadhi	समाधि	rhythmic rise and fall of verse
samataa	समता	consistency in style
sambhoga shriNgaar	संभोग श्रृंगार	see saNyoga shriNgaar
sampradaay	संप्रदाय	any school/tradition of Indian poetics
saNchaareebhaav	संचारीभाव	fleeting emotions
saNghaTan	संघटन	organisation
sannidhi	सन्निधि	absence of undue time lag between the pronunciation of one word and the next
saNskaar	संस्कार	culture
saNyoga shriNgaar	संयोग श्रृंगार	that emotion of love when the lovers are together
sarg	सर्ग	section of an epic
sattva	सत्त्व	the highest state of consciousness characterised by purity, goodness and calm; also inner strength and vigour when talking about auchitya related to composition
saukumaarya	सौकुमार्य	absence of harshness in style; tenderness of verse where something harsh is being expressed in a mild manner
saundarya	सौंदर्य	beauty
shaaNta	शांत	that rasa which evokes a freedom from all desire; equilibrium; oneness
shaashtraashrit	शास्त्राश्रित	a work based on some shaastra, or branch of knowledge
shaastra	शास्त्र	text, subject of study

shabda	शब्द	word or language
shabdaalaNkaar	शब्दालंकार	a figure of speech related to words
shabdaanupraas	शब्दानुप्रास	repetition of words
shabdashakti	शब्दशक्ति	the power of a word to convey meaning
shakti	शक्ति	the natural ability to write poetry
shleSh	श्लेष	pun
shlok	श्लोक	a poetic form used in Sanskrit, consisting of four padas or quarter-verses of eight syllables each
shobhaa	शोभा	brilliance
shriNgaar	श्रृंगार	erotic and romantic love
shrutikaTu	श्रुतिकटु	harsh sounding
smit	स्मित	slight smile
sneh	स्नेह	affection
sootra	सूत्र	formula
sphoTa	स्फोट	the concept or idea expressed by a word
sthaayibhaav	स्थायिभाव	dominant emotion
swabhaav	स्वभाव	that which is natural
swabhaavokti	स्वभावोक्ति	plain statement
swashabdavaachyataa	स्वशब्दवाच्यता	naming the emotion
taatparya vritti	तात्पर्य वृत्ति	conditions related to the meaning of a sentence
tama	तम	the lowest state of consciousness characterised by ignorance, dullness and lethargy
tanmayeekaraṇ	तन्मयीकरण	identification with the characters on the stage
ubhayaalaNkaar	उभयालंकार	a figure of speech that has properties of both shabdaalaNkaar and arthaalaNkaar
uchchhwaas	उच्छ्वास	a section in an aakhyaayikaa
udaaharaṇ	उदाहरण	example
udaarataa	उदारता	richness of expression
udaattataa	उदात्तता	an exalted style of expression

uddeepan vibhaav	उद्दीपन विभाव	cause intensifying the effect of the aalaMban vibhaav
ullaas	उल्लास	division of a book
unmeSh	उन्मेष	chapter
upahaasit	उपहासित	laughter of ridicule
upamaa	उपमा	simile
upamaan	उपमान	the thing which is compared to something else
upameya	उपमेय	the thing to which the upaaman is compared
utprekShaa	उत्प्रेक्षा	an alaNkaar comparing two things in which phrases such as 'as if' are used
vaachak	वाचक	a word giving its literal meaning
vaachyaarth	वाच्यार्थ	the literal meaning of a word
vaakya	वाक्य	sentence
vaakyavakrataa	वाक्यवक्रता	arranging padas in a sentence
vaasanaa	वासना	subconscious tendency in a person which is the result of their actions
vaatsalya	वात्सल्य	that affection that a parent has for their child
vaidarbhee reeti	वैदर्भी रीति	that reeti or diction which is primarily associated with maadhurya guṇa; is mellifluous and is ideal for all kinds of readers
vakra	वक्र	not straight
varṇaanupraas	वर्णानुप्रास	repetition of consonants
varṇavinyaasvakrataa	वर्णविन्यासवक्रता	systematic arrangement of phonemes
vastudhwani	वस्तुध्वनि	suggested meaning of an expression that has no alaNkaars
veer	वीर	the sentiment of courage
vibhaav	विभाव	the determinant of rasa
vibhakti	विभक्ति	(in Sanskrit grammar) what is added to a word to indicate its person, number, gender and case

vibhatsa	विभत्स	disgust
vichaar	विचार	thought
vichitra	विचित्र	striking, unusual
vidyaa	विद्या	art
vidyaaviruddha doSha	विद्याविरुद्ध दोष	something against the custom or principles of art
vihaasita	विहासित	gentle laughter
vipralaMbha shriNgaar	विप्रलंभ श्रृंगार	that emotion of love when the lovers are away from each other
virodhaabhaas	विरोधाभास	paradox
visarg	विसर्ग	a mark (:) placed after a noun to add the aspirated /əh/ sound to the word; for example when the (:) mark is placed after Ram, it will be pronounced 'raamaha'
viyoga shriNgaar	वियोग श्रृंगार	see vipralaMbha shriNgaar
vritti	वृत्ति	explanation
vyaahatatva	व्याहतत्व	contradiction
vyaajastuti	व्याजस्तुति	a kind of irony
vyaakaraṇ	व्याकरण	grammar
vyaapaktva	व्यापकत्व	to bloom or grow; a state of mind where there is a sudden emotional change
vyabhichaareebhaav	व्यभिचारीभाव	fleeting emotions (see saNchaareebhaav)
vyaNgyaarth	व्यंग्यार्थ	the suggested or symbolic meaning of a word
vyaNjak	व्यंजक	a word capable of a suggested or symbolic meaning
vyaNjanaa	व्यंजना	suggested meaning
vyaNjanaadhwani	व्यंजनाध्वनि	suggested meaning based on the context in which the expression has been used; may differ from reader to reader based on their understanding of the context
vyutpatti	व्युत्पत्ति	learning

yajna	यज्ञ	a sacred fire sacrifice ritual conducted in the Hindu tradition
yamak	यमक	repetition of a word which gives a different meaning each time it is repeated
yogyataa	योग्यता	the compatibility of words in a sentence
yuddhaveer	युद्धवीर	a warrior hero/person

Further Reading

Abhinavagupt. *Dhwanyalok* (Lochan Teeka), edited by Ramsagar Tripathi, Delhi, Motilal Banarsidass, 1985.

Anandwardhan. *Dhwanyalok* (Visheshwar Teeka), edited by Dr Nagendra, Varanasi, Gyanmandal, 1985.

Appaya Dikshit. *Kuvalayanand*. Mumbai, Nirnay Sagar Press, 1947.

Bhamah. *Kavyalankar*, edited by Devendra Nath Sharma, Patna, Bihar Rashtrabhasha Parishad, 1982.

Bharat. *The Natyashastra*. Translated by Monomohan Ghosh, Calcutta, Asiatic Society of Bengal, 1951.

Bhojaraja. *Shringarprakash*, edited by Rewa Prasada Dwivedi and Sadashiva Prasad Dwivedi, Indira Gandhi National Centre for the Arts, 2007.

Chaitanya, Krishna. *Sanskrit Poetics: A Critical and Comparative Study*. Mumbai, Asia Publishing House, 1965.

Dandin. *Kavyadarsh*, edited by Dharmendra Kumar Gupta, Delhi, Meharchand Laxmandas Publications, 2006.

De, S.K. *Sanskrit Poetics as a Study of Aesthetics*. U of California P, 1963.

Hira, Rajvansh Sahay. *भारतीय काव्यशास्त्र के प्रतिनिधि सिद्धांत* (*Bharatiya havyashastra ke pratinidhi Siddhant*). Varanasi, Chaukhamba, Vidya Bhawan, 1964.

Kane, P.V. *History of Sanskrit Poetics*. 4th ed., Motilal Banarsidass, 1971.

Kshemendra. *Aucityavicārcarcā*, 3rd ed., edited with commentaries by Vrajmohan Jha, Varanasi, Chaukhamba, Vidhya Bhawan, 1982.

Kuntaka. *The Vakrokti-jīvita of Kuntaka*, edited by K. Krishnamoorthy, Dharwad, Karnatak University, 1977.

Mahimbhatt. *The Vyaktiviveka of Rājānaka Srī Mahimabhaṭṭa*, edited by Rewa Prasada Dwivedi, Varanasi, Chowkhamba Sanskrit Series, 1964.

Mammat. *Kavyaprakash* (Vishweshwar Teeka), edited by Dr Nagendra, Varanasi, Gyan Mandal, 1960.

Mishra, Bhagirath. *Kavyashastra*. Varanasi, Vishwavidyalaya Prakashan, 1972.

Nagendra. *भारतीय काव्यशास्त्र की भूमिका* (*Bharatiya kavyashastra ki Bhoomika*). Delhi, National Publishing House, 1963.

Jagannath. *Rasagangadhar*. Translated by Pandit Madanmohan Jha, Varanasi, Chaukhamba Sanskrit Series, 1972.

Rajashekhar. *Kavyamimansa*. Translated by Pandit Kedarnath Sharma Saraswat, Patna, Bihar Rashtrabhasha Parishad, 1972.

Rudrat. *Kāvyālaṅkāra* (Nabhisadhu Teeka), edited by Ramdev Shukla, Varanasi, Chaukhamba, Vidya Bhawan, 1966.

Ruyyak. *Alaṁkāra Sarvasva* (Vimarshin Teeka). Translated by Rewa Prasada Dwivedi, Varanasi, Chaukhamba Sanskrit Series, 1971.

Shukla, Usha. *भारतीय काव्यशास्त्र* (*Bharatiya kavyashastra*). Bhopal, Kailash Pustak Sadan, 2016.

Agni Purana. Gorakhpur, Gita Press, 2016.

Vaman. *The Kāvyalṅkār Sūtras of Vāmana*. Translated by Ganganath Jha, Delhi, Sri Satguru Publications, 1990.

Vijayavardhana, G. *An Outline of Sanskrit Poetics*. Varanasi, Chaukhamba Sanskrit Series, 1970.

Vishwanath. *Sahitya darpan: Sri vishwanath kavirajkrutaha*. Translated by Shaligram Shastri, Delhi, Motilal Banarsidass, 2009.

About the Authors

Dr Ravi Nandan Sinha was Director, Xavier Research Centre, St. Xavier's College (Autonomous), Ranchi till his sudden passing in 2021. He was Associate Professor and Head, Postgraduate Department of English, St. Xavier's College (Autonomous), Ranchi where he taught undergraduate and postgraduate classes for over forty years. He also taught Indian poetics to MA English students for ten years. He has over fifteen books to his credit including *A Handful of Sand* (a translation of Gurdial Singh's *Rete di ikk mutthi*), *Rhapsodies* (a book of poetry) and other works on literary criticism and translation. He was a Jury Member on the Translation Awards committee of the Sahitya Akademi, New Delhi. He was also an experienced editor and had been editing *The Quest* since 1987.

Dr Narendra Kumar 'Pathak' has Masters degrees in Sanskrit and Hindi and received his PhD in the study of Hindi and Sanskrit drama. He taught Sanskrit at St. Xavier's College (Autonomous) Ranchi as an Assistant Professor of Sanskrit for twenty-one years. A person of wide interests, he has also been associated with All India Radio, Ranchi as an assignment-based approved voice announcer since 1987. He has rich experience in the fields of journalism and literature and has worked as an editorial associate in print media.